The Worship Leader's Handbook

PRACTICAL ANSWERS TO TOUGH QUESTIONS

Tom Kraeuter

Training Resources • Hillsboro, Missouri

Emerald Books

P.O. Box 635
Lynnwood, Washington 98046

by Tom Kraeuter

All Scripture quotations are from either the King James Version or
The Holy Bible, New International Version, copyright © 1973, 1978,
1984 International Bible Society. Used by permission of Zondervan
Bible Publishers.

The Worship Leader's Handbook
© 1997 Training Resources, Inc.
8929 Old LeMay Ferry Road
Hillsboro, MO 63050
(314) 789-4522

Dedication

I humbly dedicate this book to my mother, Ruth Kraeuter. Thanks, Mom, for teaching me right from wrong, but especially for loving me even when I chose wrong. I love you!

Thanks to:

Jon Bergt for much of the information (and even the wording) on pages 25 and 26. Jon, you articulated it much better than I could have.

Kent Henry for the impetus to begin this book.

Jennifer Brody, for another whiz-bang job of editing. Your talent for making me sound like I know what I'm talking about is amazing! Thanks!

The thousands of worship leaders across North America who have attended our worship seminars and asked these questions. Keep pressing on!

My wonderful family for allowing me the time to learn, write, teach and follow God's call. I love you, Barbara, David, Stephen and Amy!

Other books by Tom Kraeuter

*Keys to Becoming
an Effective Worship Leader*

Developing an Effective Worship Ministry

*Things They Didn't Teach Me
in Worship Leading School*

Worship Is... What?!

*If Standing Together Is So Great,
Why Do We Keep Falling Apart?*

Table of Contents

Section 4: Leading Worship

Section 5: Songs

Section 6: Relationship to the Pastor and the Congregation

Section 7: The Music/Worship Team

Appendix

Preface

In teaching worship seminars across North America, I consistently ask those in attendance to write down specific questions they have about worship and leading worship. Later in the seminar I endeavor to answer as many of those as time permits. From this experience, as well as my six years with *Psalmist* magazine, I have seen certain topics come up again and again. These are the questions that I have attempted to address in this publication.

Please note that throughout this book the phrases "worship ministry," "praise team," "church music ministry," etc., are frequently interchanged. Although you might differentiate certain aspects of the music ministry in your church (i.e., choir, instrumentalists, main vocalists, etc.), I see each of these as part of the whole. As such, most of the information herein would be applicable to any or all of these.

The format of this book is question and answer. To the straight-through reader some of the information may appear repetitious. This is simply because it seemed best to have the answer to each question stand alone for easy, practical reference. By doing this there is no need for constant cross-referencing to other questions. Each is self contained. My hope is that this book will be used often as a helpful guide for those tough worship leading situations.

This is certainly not meant to be the final word on these varied topics. Honestly, one of my major frustrations over the years has been that the Bible is very silent on most of the practical aspects of leading worship. There are many general biblical concepts that can be applied to the role of worship leading, but when it comes to specifics, there is little scriptural help. Because of this, many of the things shared in this book are from my experience and background. Although I have led worship for more than 20 years and in practically every type of denominational or non-denominational church imaginable, these answers are very often simply my opinions. (I think they are really good opinions, but they are still just my opinions.) I submit them to you in all humility, in hope that they will help you avoid some of the pitfalls into which I have frequently stumbled.

My prayer for you is that you would continue to increase in the gifts and abilities which God has placed in you. In all that you do may you bring glory and honor to the One Who is worthy.

Section 1

Worship Foundations

How important is the overall lifestyle of those involved in the ministry of praise and worship?

This question has undoubtedly been the topic of numerous books and articles over the years. There is no way I could do it justice in the space available here, but let me offer a few thoughts.

First, leading praise and worship requires that there be an ongoing relationship with the Lord. The role of the worship leader is not primarily musical. It is, first and foremost, spiritual. You will not be able to effectively lead worship over the long-term if you do not have a personal worship relationship with God. This means consistent Bible study and prayer. It also means seeking the Lord and His guidance for your life, business, family and ministry decisions.

You can not take people where you have not been. If you are not regularly involved in worshipping God in your personal devotion time then you will ultimately not be able to lead others in worship. Your relationship with the Lord is the thing that will make leading worship possible. Without that as part of your life, no amount of talent, practice, or mental and physical preparation will help.

Those involved in the ministry of praise and worship should have lives that reflect worship in all they do and say. Their attitude should be "...whatever you do, do it all for the glory of God" (1 Corinthians 10:31).

Secondly, how you act in public, outside of church, is very important. Anyone who is regularly standing before the congregation in any ministry capacity is seen as a leader by those in the congregation. I was the bass player in our church when I first recognized this fact. People saw me in front of the church week after week and therefore identified me as a leader in the church. My attitude was, "Wrong! I'm just the bass player." But it didn't matter what I said to them. In their minds the fact that I was seen in ministry on a regular basis identified me as a leader.

The same is true in nearly every church. Anyone who is up front ministering regularly is seen as a leader. Because of this their actions outside of church can be crucial. People see them at a park playing with their children and think, "That's what a worshipping Christian is like." Or they encounter them at the local discount store, yelling at the manager because of some ongoing problem, and think, "Oh, that's what a worshipping Christian is like."

Obviously, it is unrealistic to expect perfection from people. However, for anyone in any leadership capacity, the standards are higher. Qualifications for overseers and deacons are listed in 1 Timothy 3. It is safe to assume that not everyone involved in the ministry of praise and worship will be an overseer or a deacon, but they are still in some sort of leadership role. Because of this, a higher standard of lifestyle is required.

In all of this, a life of pure and simple devotion to Christ (2 Corinthians 11:3) is essential. More than fantastic musical abilities or a great memory for song lyrics, a life that reflects a sincere worship of God is vital.

My church is just coming into praise and worship. Having been the music director at this church for many years I have seen that new ideas and programs need to be instituted every few years to keep boredom and complacency from setting in. What will I do in two or three years when the newness of these praise and worship choruses is gone?

Today's praise and worship movement has at least a couple of inherent safeguards built into it. First, the song selection is consistently being renewed. New songs are being written regularly and are added to the church repertoire. Even the style of music is "evolving" to be current with trends in society. These things will continue, making praise and worship songs less of a "program" and more of a constantly renewed resource.

Beyond this, praise and worship is ultimately not just a Sunday morning experience. It must become part of the everyday life of believers to be valid.

It is very obvious that a life full of worship and praise has tremendous impact on our daily struggles. Even in the midst of major trials, David, the psalmist, consistently set his heart to worship God throughout his life. As a result he repeatedly saw the Lord's power and victory.

Paul and Silas sang praises to God while in prison (Acts 16:25). That was certainly not a corporate, Sunday morning gathering. The writer of Hebrews tells us, "...let us continually offer to God a sacrifice of praise—the fruit of lips that confess

His Name" (Hebrews 13:15). "Continually" does not mean just in the church building when everyone else is there. Psalm 34:1 says: "I will bless the Lord at all times." There is no addendum to that statement that says, "...but mostly on Sunday morning." You get the picture.

Our worship and praise of almighty God must go way beyond the Sunday morning singing experience. When our focus is on the Lord throughout the week, our focus will be automatically on Him on Sunday morning. When praise and worship become a part of life for the believers we will no longer need to worry about another new fad to keep them interested. God is never dull. If their main point of focus is Him, they won't become bored.

One other note: don't forget to pray and seek the Lord for your church and your area of ministry. The living God is far more than a program. He has promised never to leave us (Hebrews 13:5), and He said that He will build His church (Matthew 16:18). Trust His promises and keep following Him.

A recent guest minister at our church was giving an altar call. In his appeal he stated that there would be no "musical hype" as in many churches: "I don't want emotionalism to affect your decision." What do you think about this?

In saying this, the minister seemed to miss some fundamental principles regarding music and worship. Throughout Scripture God repeatedly shows the importance of music and its effect on people. Far more than just "hype," music is a powerful force that can have dramatic impact on people. If we can grasp a few of these valuable scriptural principles, we will be better able to utilize music to its fullest potential.

First, the Lord often manifests His presence in a more tangible way through music and praise. Psalm 22:3 says that God inhabits the praises of His people. We hear a lot about this concept today. This idea almost seems overused. But remember that even overuse does not negate the truth of it. God really does inhabit our praises, and when He "shows up" anything can happen in people's lives. We ought not take His presence "enthroned on our praises" for granted.

Music played by someone whose heart is turned toward the Lord can have strong spiritual impact. Just as David's harp music impacted King Saul (1 Samuel 16:23), so our music can today. The evil spirit tormenting King Saul fled as David played. God is no respecter of persons (Acts 10:34). What happened through David can happen through us. Oppressive spirits causing physical ailments and/or mental anguish will flee as our music and worship flow from pure hearts. This obviously goes well beyond the stage of musical hype.

Also, music and praise seem somehow to release the miracle-working power of God. Remember Paul and Silas in jail? (Acts 16:22-30). As they prayed and sang the earth shook and the doors of the jail were opened. In 2 Chronicles 20 Jehoshaphat sent "those who sang to the Lord and those who praised Him in holy attire" out ahead of the army. "And when they began singing and praising, the Lord set ambushes against (their enemies)" (2 Chronicles 20:22). Today, through our music and praise, we too can see a strong spiritual impact. This would certainly not be classified as emotionalism.

As a practical/technical note, music seems to help focus people's attention toward the matter at hand. In photography this is known as the focal point. You may focus on one element in the picture, but all the surrounding elements are included. In a similar way, music helps achieve a focal point for the congregation. It is not hype but a vehicle or tool that God has given us to aid the building of His kingdom and draw people to look to Him.

Finally, we must also understand, affirm and accept the role of those who lead in music and worship. There is much scriptural precedent for receiving a person in their given office (Matthew 10:40-42). We should not quench their ministry by seeing them as those who provide only background music and emotionalism. A music leader who truly understands his role before God and the people will add much power and life to the ministry.

Having said all of this, it should be noted that there is a fine line between using music for honest, godly purposes and using it to manipulate people. The real issue is in the motivation of your heart. Are you endeavoring to give people a setting whereby they can connect with God? Or are you trying to manipulate a spiritual experience? Honestly answering these questions is very important because God is always more interested in our hearts than our actions.

God has placed tremendous potential within music. When used incorrectly it has the ability to mislead and deceive. But when used according to God's plan, music has real spiritual power to be a vehicle to help transform lives.

Is it necessary to always have a feeling of God's presence or a high level of emotion when you praise and worship or do you sometimes just praise and worship out of obedience?

No, you may not always have a strong sensing of the presence of God or a high level of emotion during a time of praise and worship. Seeking after such feelings is a trap into which many believers fall. Because they once experienced a strong excitement or even an honest encounter with the Lord, they now desire that same feeling above everything else. There are Christians today who go from meeting to meeting, looking for their next spiritual high. The truth is that there is little real difference between these people and a chronic drug addict. Their lives revolve around getting their next "fix."

I am not trying to negate any type of emotion. As human beings part of our make-up is emotions. God has given us emotions for a reason. However, emotions are not the thing that initiated my relationship with the Lord, and long-term, they will not keep me going. We may sometimes have a high level of emotions during a time of praise and worship, but not always. Worshipping and praising God is far more than just an emotional experience.

A couple of years ago I attended a conference where the main speaker shared an applicable insight about this. It happened that he and a friend visited a church on Sunday morning while they were traveling. As they left, the friend confided that although he had enjoyed the sermon, he really hadn't gotten anything out of the worship time. The man looked at his friend and asked, "Have you ever wondered what that's got to do with anything?" His point was obvious: Who is the worship for? It's not ultimately for us. It's for God.

I realize that we often receive during worship. Sometimes, if we are struggling in life, it can be very beneficial to focus on God, to worship Him. Doing this can alter our perspective and cause a change in us. We have received through worship. However, that is still not the *primary* focus. Too often we have the selfish what's-in-it-for-me mentality instead of simply worshipping our God because He is worthy and desires fellowship with us.

Ironically, even as we learn to focus more on our worthy God, we find our own emotional needs met more and more. For example, when my wife and I first started dating and moved toward the direction of marriage, I thought mostly about whether she could meet my needs. Now, almost 20 years into our marriage, I find myself more and more trying to meet her needs. Yet in doing so, I find my needs met all the more — not because I'm trying to get those needs met, but because I am giving myself to her. The same is true in worship. The more I wholeheartedly give myself to God in worship, the more I will receive. Meeting my needs is still not my primary focus, but it will happen.

We need to make a decision before we ever start into a time of corporate worship and praise. We must resolve to worship the Lord whether we feel anything or not. Our attitude should be, "God, if I don't feel anything here today, I will still worship You because You are still worthy."

When we honestly make this decision from our hearts, then we can enjoy the emotions because they are in their proper perspective. Our feelings are not the main issue; they are a side issue. The main concern is that we are there to honor our King.

There are even times when it is necessary for us simply to offer up a sacrifice of praise. When our feelings and emotions are lacking, it can truly be a sacrifice. However, we can honor the Lord just as much (and perhaps more so) when we have no emotional excitement, but only a deep-seated commitment to worship our always-worthy God.

Is there a difference between praise and worship?

In recent years much has been taught about the supposed differences between praise and worship. Praise is generally referred to as preparatory, more jubilant and even light-natured. It is usually seen as more exuberant and loud, a preliminary. Worship, on the other hand, is said to be the goal. It is supposedly more somber and reverent and of higher purpose. It should, by its very nature, be more intimate and quiet. Many passages of Scripture support these ideas. However, there are also many that do not.

Psalm 66:1 speaks of much expressive praise, loud and glorious. Then verse 4 says: "All the earth will worship Thee, and will sing praises to Thy Name." Here praise is occurring after or perhaps during worship.

In 2 Chronicles 20:18-19, the king (Jehoshaphat) and the whole assembly fell down and worshipped, but then the Levites stood up to praise loudly! That doesn't quite fit the concept either.

In 2 Chronicles 29:28-30, the folks are apparently really confused. They start out worshipping in verses 27 and 28, but the description with all the singing and trumpets sounds more like praise. Then they bow in worship in verse 29. Then in verse 30 they go back to singing praise and then back again into worship!

In Revelation 19:4, the four creatures and 24 elders fall down and worship God. Then in verse 5 a voice says, "Give praise to our God..." and a huge multitude responds in verses

6-8 by shouting and rejoicing, "Hallelujah." Why praise when they've already entered into worship? Is heaven confused? Apparently in the Scripture the order is not necessarily always the same as what we have been taught.

When I was in seminary many years ago, one of the professors gave us an assignment. We were to do a word study on the words "praise" and "worship." The plan was to look up all of the times either of those words are used in our English Bibles and see what the original Greek or Hebrew words literally meant. The goal was to see if there was a consistency to the original understanding of those two words.

A week later, everyone had completed the assignment and we shared our results. I was amazed that nearly everyone in the class had arrived at the same conclusions. Praise, according to the original understanding, is predominantly something we say or sing; it is vocal in expression. Worship, overall, is generally something we do; it is physical in expression. The original Greek and Hebrew words that we translate "praise" have definitions like "declare" and "bless." The original words for "worship" literally mean things like "bow down" or "kiss the hand toward."

Please realize that even these definitions are not always true. There are a couple of scriptural references that violate even this concept. However, from a biblical perspective, a much stronger case can be made for these definitions than for the ideas I shared at the beginning of this section.

To me the bottom line is this: We spend far too much time analyzing what we're doing and not enough time actually doing it. Let's just honor, adore, glorify, exalt — praise and worship — our ever-worthy God and not be so concerned about labeling exactly what we are doing.

Section 2

The Worship Leader

When I'm leading worship I have trouble concentrating on the Lord. Is this normal?

It does seem to be "normal" in the sense that many people have the same problem. On the other hand, I don't believe that it is God's best. Let's look at some of the hindrances that cause us to struggle in this area.

One of the most common causes of not being able to worship while leading is lack of familiarity with the music. It is difficult (at best) to concentrate on the Lord when you are concentrating on your music. To help this you must work at the music on a consistent basis. This means practicing the songs (in the various keys you will be using, including modulations), practicing chord progressions, performing technical work with your instrument and voice, studying further in music theory, etc. All of this sounds like a lot of work, but there is no way around this technical aspect. Without this basic foundation in place you will always struggle with the music.

Another common problem is lack of preparation. If you don't know where you are going you will have great difficulty getting there. As a worship leader you need to have a plan (preferably in conjunction with the pastor) as to the direction of the service. In this way your leading will be more focused and less of the hit-and-miss concept. Remember: it's perfectly alright to plan ahead. God can guide and direct you just as easily (if not more so) before the service as He can during it.

A third common area is lack of personal worship in private. You cannot do in front of people on Sunday mornings what is missing from your private life. If you worship God on your own Monday through Saturday, your worship will flow more easily on Sunday. Seeing praise and worship as a lifestyle is a real key to effectively leading praise and worship.

Finally, when all of the tangible things are taken care of, sometimes there still seems to be a lack of worship. In humility of heart, submit it to the Lord. Realize that you have done all that you can and ask Him to work that worship in you.

I am often so concerned about getting everything to flow properly and with leading others in worship that sometimes I feel like I missed actually worshipping God. Any suggestions?

?

Some people would tell you that this is okay. I have heard speakers at worship conferences teach that the worship leader doesn't need to worship while he's leading. They say he can worship later, at home, by himself. They insist that his primary focus while leading is to be certain that the people connect with the Lord.

I have also heard the opposite taught: that the worship leader must focus totally on God. "Don't worry about the people," I've heard. "The people will follow if you are worshipping."

The title, worship leader, implies that both of these are only partially true. It is vital that the worship leader actually worship while leading, but if he becomes so completely "lost in God" that he forgets about the people, then he has missed part of his responsibility. On the other hand, if he is so focused on the people that he misses worshipping the Lord, then he has also missed a major part of his role.

Ultimately, the worship leader must strike a balance between leading the people and worshipping God himself. Exactly how to do this is a difficult question to answer because each service will be different.

Some practical suggestions are:

1. Seek the Lord ahead of time for His direction for the service, asking the Holy Spirit to guide you.

2. Plan the service, including songs, Scriptures, etc., based on the leading of the Holy Spirit.

3. Practice the music just the way you intend to do it in the service.

4. Commit your plans to the Lord and ask Him to make up any lack in you and your abilities.

Having made all of these practical preparations you should find it much easier to worship during the corporate worship time.

I am a person with virtually no musical training, yet I am a worship leader in a local congregation. I am able to effectively lead people in worship, but sometimes it is difficult for me to make up for my lack of knowledge in music. Others on our worship team have more talent and training than I, but have been unable to lead effectively. Any advice?

Musical training is not the foremost criteria for being a worship leader. It is only one of several major considerations. Other serious factors would include clarifying your calling, being recognized and appointed by your local church leadership to the position of worship leader, and having organizational, planning and even interpersonal relational skills. Proficiency with your voice and instrument are also important. Let me expand on each of these.

Calling

There is a tremendous difference between having musical abilities or talents and having been "called" by God. There is no doubt that the Lord can use natural and learned skills. These are important and should be developed. But the real issue is that God calls certain people to tasks even before their natural abilities are equal to the task. Jeremiah was a youth when God called him to be a prophet. Moses was tending sheep when the Lord instructed him to rescue Israel. Peter was an unlearned fisherman that God used to bring thousands to the saving knowledge of Jesus. These are just a few examples of this truth.

Discerning whether you are called can include many factors. The desire in your heart and confirmation from those close to you as well as the local church leadership, can all be important criteria for determining if you are indeed called to a particular area of service.

Keep in mind that even though something may not be your life-long calling, sometimes God may have you serve in a particular capacity for a season. The reasons for this can be varied. Perhaps you may help the church through a transitional period. Maybe it will help you determine (or prepare you for) the real calling on your life. Whatever the reason, always maintain a servant attitude.

Recognition and Appointment

You should also realize that it is within your church leadership's scriptural authority to recognize and appoint the people deemed spiritually qualified for leadership roles. Without this recognition from a local church you may declare yourself to be a worship leader but you have no real authority for leading.

Ultimately, if the church leadership does recognize the gift and calling and sets you in place, you may not be as musically qualified as some of the other musicians and singers, but the leadership is comfortable with your abilities to fulfill this role. You need to attend to this position as a good steward of a godly opportunity, serving to the best of your ability.

Leadership Skills

Many deficiencies can be compensated for if you excel in this area. Those who excel as musicians or singers but lack leadership skills have a different position within the music team.

Allow those with gifts in your areas of deficiency to help you. For example, a gifted instrumentalist on your team may be able to suggest the best key range and specific chords for a given song. One of your singers may be able to give input regarding the individual parts the singers should be working on. You may be able to utilize these people in your rehearsals to more effectively communicate in their area of expertise. Good leaders are always looking for ways to utilize the skills of their people.

By planning ahead and communicating well, you will be able to overcome your limitations. First seek God for the direction and theme of the upcoming meeting/service and choose songs that seem appropriate for that setting. Then meet with your main instrumentalist to work out key ranges and modulations ahead of time so that the flow is not hindered.

Interpersonal Relational Skills

This area is at least partly included in the leadership skills mentioned above, but it also goes beyond this. Interacting with those in the music ministry on a personal basis, showing care and concern for their lives will go a long way toward encouraging them to follow you as a leader.

In essence what I am really saying here is that you pastor those involved in the music ministry. Please understand that I am not saying that you officially become a pastor in the church nor even that you be given the title "pastor." The important thing is that you care for the people. Let them know that you are really interested in them as people.

This even goes beyond just those involved in the music ministry. When the people in the congregation sense a genuine care and concern from you, they are much more willing to follow your leadership.

Musical Skills

I would highly recommend that you begin improving your musical ability and knowledge. You should pursue individualized instruction (vocal and/or instrumental). Find a teacher that is able to instruct you in what you want to know (i.e. someone geared totally to classical music will not be of significant help if you want to learn a more contemporary style of music). Take a praise and worship tape of the musical style you want to learn and ask the instructor if he can teach you that style of music. Consider going back to school to learn some of the basics of music theory. This can be done at a local junior college or university. You can usually apply to audit these classes for a small registration fee.

Understanding each of these various aspects of being a worship leader should help you overcome your lack of musical expertise.

As a fledgling musician, how can I fully worship and not be so into the mechanics of the music?

I have probably been asked this question dozens of times and my answer is always the same: practice. The more familiar you are with the music prior to the "performance" of the music, the easier it will be for you. If you have gone over a difficult chord change or an unusual progression many times in practice, it will come much more naturally when you do it on Sunday morning.

People often appear disappointed after I answer this question. It appears that they were looking for an easy answer. They want the solution that won't cause them work. There is a lady on the music team at my home church who is a fabulous sight-reader. She can sight-read practically anything, either singing or playing. Several years ago I commented that I would give my right arm to be able to do that. She responded, "Will you give me a couple hours a week?" I wanted the easy solution. Hers was much more realistic.

Most things that are worth having are worth working for. Work at your music. Practice those songs at home. Be diligent. Then, during the times of leading worship, you will have much less of a struggle with the mechanics and will be able to focus more on worshipping God.

Some people say that I seem really inhibited in leading worship. How can I overcome this?

I will offer some thoughts on the how-to-overcome-this in a moment, but first let me preface those ideas with an important comment: As much as possible, don't allow others to dictate how you should act or not act. You shouldn't attempt to fit into someone else's image of a worship leader. Instead, simply be yourself. Long-term people will recognize the difference between what is genuine and what is contrived or produced for the sake of the onlookers.

One of the main reasons that people sometimes feel somewhat inhibited while leading worship is that much of what is done is unnatural to them. The religious background I came out of taught me to be very inhibited concerning demonstrative praise and worship. Singing, kneeling, sitting or standing had to be done at just the right time. So when I first started leading worship I wasn't certain that I believed, at least to the point of exemplifying it, what I saw in the Word of God about freedom in praise and worship. I saw celebrating, dancing, shouting and all sorts of other expressions of worship. These were all new, and more than a little scary to me. It took time in the Word and time watching other people to help rid myself of wrong ideas and beliefs about acceptable ways to praise and worship the Lord. You need to see it in the Word, believe it in your heart, and then, finally, step out and do it. For these expressions to be a natural part of leading worship they must become a natural part of daily life. It is difficult to lead others in an area which is unfamiliar to you.

Those things which we do in public should simply be an extension of what we do our private times with the Lord. Often I have found myself shouting to the Lord with a voice of triumph or kneeling before the Lord in my personal prayer times. I wasn't doing it because I was a part of a worship team or because people were watching. It was the genuine expression of my heart at that moment to the Lord.

The more we do anything the more comfortable we become with it, whether alone or in front of others. Maintain a regular worship time with the Lord on an individual basis. This will help you grow out of your inhibitions and into honest expressions of praise and worship.

Lack of preparation can also cause people to seem inhibited. You will have more freedom in praise and worship if you go in with a plan of what to do. Know where you are going and you will be much more at ease while you are leading.

Finally, be yourself. Don't try to put on a show. Just be you. Worshippers don't want a show, they want to worship. Ask God to work in you those qualities that He wants there. "If therefore the Son shall make you free, you shall be free indeed" (John 8:36).

I'm the new worship leader at our church and it seems like everyone wants me to be like the former worship leader. Should I conform?

In nearly any area of leadership, most people who replace someone else will have to endure a season of comparisons of their "performance" to that of the former person. It is not fun or easy, but you may take comfort in the fact that it usually does not last a long time.

I went through this in my situation. When I replaced the man who had been leading worship at our church for ten years it was a difficult transition. There were constant comparisons to my leading and his leading. For a while, I was seen by some as being lower caliber than my predecessor. Having now been the main worship leader for over a dozen years, those who lead in my absence sometimes face the same type of comparisons.

Some churches use this understanding as the basis for having a rotating schedule for multiple worship leaders. Unfortunately, the comparisons will still be there. The people may not be overt or crass about it, but they will still have their favorites. Making such comparisons appears to be natural human nature.

To answer your question directly then: yes and no. Yes, you should glean from all of the positive vision and direction of the former worship leader. If there is a music program already in existence, you do not need to start everything over from scratch. Do not recreate a new program for the sake of saying that it is yours.

On the other hand, obviously, you as a person are not exactly like the former worship leader. You can not and should not be exactly like him.

Perhaps it would be helpful to make a list of the items that people suggest you should consider. Then, with your pastor, pray and look at the list together. There will be certain things that, because of personality, background, etc., are obviously not you. You will both probably agree that these items are unworkable. In a mature manner, look at the remaining items trying to see what is worth considering. Set goals and make plans as to how to implement any needed changes.

The important thing is not that you become like (or refuse to consider becoming like) the former worship leader. The most important issue is finding what you believe the Lord wants, and hence, what is the best for the congregation.

I have trouble worshipping when I am not leading. Why is this and how do I overcome it?

Some years ago I heard a worship leader speaking at a conference. He asked a question at the beginning of his teaching session: "What would you do or what would your reaction be if your pastor came to you and said, 'From now on we are not going to have praise and worship as we have known it. We are going to sing only two or three hymns accompanied by just the piano'?"

My mind raced to formulate an answer to his question, but before I could adequately pull my thoughts together he said, "That happened at our church... and it was the right thing to do." He went on to explain that the musicians had begun to see worship as emanating from their musical abilities, from their instruments. When they were asked to sit with the rest of the congregation during worship, they didn't know what to do. They didn't know how to worship without their instruments.

It is easy for us to get caught up in the musical aspects of praise and worship, but God is far more interested in our hearts.

I would highly recommend that you daily spend time worshipping God privately. Speak and sing your praises to the Lord with no musical accompaniment. Don't worry about emotions or feelings. Make it a sacrifice of praise if you need to. Just do it.

Along with this, go to meetings where you are not leading. Express your gratitude, praise, thanksgiving, worship and adoration to the Lord, without the trappings of being up front.

In all of these be sure to focus less on the leading/performance aspect and more on worshipping the Lord. Yes, He wants our praises to be beautiful (technically correct), but more than this, God wants our hearts.

The important point in all of this is that what we do in leading others in worship should not be an end in and of itself. It should flow out of a life that is filled with worship to God. Apart from this, our leading has little or no value.

How important is it for me as a worship leader to train others? How should I go about this discipleship process?

The trendy term today is mentoring. Whatever terminology you use — discipling, training others, mentoring — make sure you do it.

Ephesians 4:11-12 says that one of the functions of church leadership is to "equip the saints for work of the ministry." In light of this, my job as a worship leader is not just to lead worship. My job is to train others in leading worship. Equipping the saints for the work of the ministry.

Most worship leaders do not seem to see training others as a high priority. Of course, it is necessary to lead worship for corporate gatherings, to find new songs and to oversee the worship team. These are all important. But beyond all of these we must draw others into the gifts that God has put into them. By doing this we are beginning to fulfill what He told us to do.

Most churches (even large churches) have one worship leader. If that person is absent for any reason, it is often assumed that the worship segment of the service will be lacking. Is this really necessary? Not if we will disciple others to lead worship.

I am not suggesting that you have several people leading with no one person in charge. That can be an extremely difficult situation. What is needed is a worship leader who will disciple others into leading.

At my church I am the primary worship leader. But through careful and deliberate personal instruction, I have trained and taught others in leading worship. Some of them have moved on to lead worship at other churches. Some are still at our church as part of our worship team and they take over the leadership role when I am absent (even sometimes when I am still there).

We have sat and discussed various aspects of worship and worship leading. We have prayed together. I have attempted to answer their worship leading questions. Each one is as thoroughly prepared to lead as I can make them before they take on a Sunday morning worship service.

They have each "taken the big plunge" on a Sunday morning when I was present. I did this deliberately so I could act as a back-up in case of an "emergency." In this way, they are able to concentrate more on their worship leading instead of on any potential problems.

After the service, I offer my thoughts, a constructive analysis, on what they did. My objective is to give creative, practical input which will help them the next time. I also offer lots of encouragement. This last point is vital. I even tend to give praise to them in front of the rest of the team or sometimes even the congregation. Timely encouragement will usually have better long-term results than even practical criticism.

It should be noted that I do not claim to know all there is to know about leading worship. I simply trust that the Holy Spirit within them will make up for what I cannot offer... and He does! The point is this: we need to disciple others even if we do not "have it all together." If you wait until you are perfect, it will never get done.

If you do not have what you consider a good candidate for leading worship, then ask God to send someone (or to show you the person who is already there). It is always amazing to see how faithful the Lord is when we really trust Him.

In all of this, remember that there are those who will simply be musicians or singers, not leaders. Don't downplay the role of these people: they are important. But continue to look for those faithful people to whom you can entrust leadership, those who will also be able to teach others (2 Timothy 2:2).

Remember, if God has given you a position of authority in His church, it is not just so you can do all the work. Disciple others. It is not just a good idea... He commands it.

Is it normal to be totally exhausted after leading worship on Sunday morning?

I am not certain as to whether it is normal but it does seem to be quite common. Many worship leaders experience this. Realistically, several factors may contribute to this exhaustion.

First, often worship leaders spend a great deal of time preparing for a service. When I am preparing to lead worship it is not unusual for me to be up past my normal bedtime on Saturday night and then rise earlier than usual on Sunday morning. This less-than-the-normal-amount of sleep can certainly be a contributing factor to being very tired on Sunday afternoon.

Along with this, there can also be the mental strain involved in leading worship. You must always be mentally alert, thinking ahead to what is coming next and considering what to say between songs and how to say it. All of these can ultimately be very taxing. They can cause a measure of fatigue.

Additionally, there can be physical factors such as the adrenaline rush that can occur in leading worship. After having been pumped full of a natural stimulant for the duration of the up-front time, your body's normal reaction is to enter a state of tremendous relaxation.

All of these various things combined can certainly lead to feeling totally exhausted after the service. Don't worry, though. Someone recently told me that "saint" (the word frequently used in Scripture for the followers of Jesus) is an acronym: Sunday Afternoon Is Nap Time. :-)

Section 3

Preparing to Lead

My pastor does not want me to prepare ahead of time *(make a song list) for leading worship. He feels it is better to "follow the Holy Spirit" by being spontaneous. Any comments?*

The idea that being spontaneous is equal to following the Holy Spirit has been widely propagated in the church today. The truth is that this idea is not found in the Bible. Nowhere does Scripture suggest that spontaneity is a guarantee that the Holy Spirit is leading. In fact, I have seen many spontaneous things happen that were clearly not God-directed.

The Bible also does not tell us that we cannot be led by God when planning ahead. In fact, if we look honestly at Scripture, we find just the opposite. The Lord Himself had a plan from the beginning of time for the redemption of mankind. It was not a last-minute thought. God did not wake up one morning and say, "Gosh, Son, look at the mess they've made. What are we going to do?!" No, He had it planned from the foundation of the earth (Revelation 13:8).

You probably recall the time in 2 Chronicles 20 when God's people were about to be attacked by three foreign nations. King Jehoshaphat sent the singers out ahead of the army praising the Lord. Do you know why he did that? Because, under the leadership of Jehoshaphat, the people sought God about what they were to do, and He clearly told them that He would win the battle for them. They did not wait for a spontaneous word in the midst of battle — they asked the Lord beforehand.

There are numerous other scriptural examples of this same thing happening. The important thing to remember is that being led by the Spirit simply means that God is guiding. It does not always have to be an immediate spontaneous revelation for the situation in which you are involved. God can give you guidance ahead of time just like He did for Jehoshaphat. I'm convinced that God knows what He wants to accomplish on a given Sunday morning by at least Saturday night — maybe even sooner. And if we will ask Him, He will tell us.

We too frequently picture God as the big, celestial Cart-Driver in the sky who holds the carrot just beyond our reach. That is certainly not His heart. God is not in the business of frustrating His servants. If He calls us to do something, He will equip us to do it.

In planning for a given service, then, we must always remember that our number one priority is to seek God's guidance. Do not get caught in the trap of simply relying on what has worked in the past. Without a fresh understanding of the Lord's will for a given service we are really just going through the motions.

Please understand that I am certainly not ruling out any type of spontaneity. The truth is that some spontaneity can be good. Although I always have a prepared list of songs for a service, I do not always know how many times we will do each song, or how many times we'll repeat the last line of a particular song, or what I will say in between certain songs. I may even add an unplanned song or eliminate a planned one. After 20 years of leading worship I am very comfortable sensing the response of the congregation and allowing that to dictate some of those variables.

Another important consideration is that a music/worship

leader can only be spontaneous to his level of musical proficiency. He cannot be expected to lead a song with which he is unfamiliar or which he cannot handle musically. The repertoire of the average church is between 200 and 400 songs. To memorize this many songs accurately, especially for a volunteer or part-time worship leader, is a monumental task.

Besides the worship leader having a list, this planning is also very helpful for others involved in the music ministry. Very few churches, especially smaller ones, have the luxury of a team of musicians who can all play extremely well by ear. Because of this it is very beneficial for them to have music for the songs. If they must page through 300 songs to find the right one, they might not be ready to play until the song is over. Obviously, some proficiency in playing by ear is a good idea in case there is a deviation from the song list, but to expect everyone to play every song by ear or from memory is unrealistic.

Following the Lord is not the same as being spontaneous. Ask Him to guide you and He will.

How important is it to have a theme for the worship time? For example, worshipping God as our Rock (stability) or Jesus as our coming King.

?

Some churches are very insistent about having a theme. They feel that everything in the service should help lead people along a single path. The music, the prayers, the sermon — everything —are all geared toward a specific theme.

Personally, I approach the idea of having a theme differently if the main part of the worship is going to be before the sermon than I do if the main worship time will be after the sermon. I view these two time slots very differently.

If the main time of praise and worship will be prior to the sermon, my objective is simply to get people to focus on the Lord. In doing so they become open to what He wants to do in their hearts and lives. It is sometimes likened to preparing the ground before the seed is sown. The worship ministry team plows the soil of the hearts so that the sower, the preacher, can plant the seed.

Again, my primary focus is to get the people to look to God. I am not interested in "preaching" (through my song selection or sharing between songs) the pastor's message before he does. If the congregation honestly focuses on the Lord, they will be ready to receive what He wants to give them during the sermon.

However, if the main praise and worship segment will be after the sermon, I tend to be much more theme-oriented. Once the sermon has been given, it can be very beneficial to reinforce that message with thematic songs. This can help drive home the point in a powerful way.

A sermon about God's love can be followed by songs giving thanks for that love. A message concerning the second-coming of Jesus could be reinforced with songs about our expectant anticipation of His coming. In this way we can strengthen the point of the sermon and make it more memorable for the people.

I have heard that a biblical pattern, such as Psalm 95, should be followed in leading worship. What do you think about this idea?

I, too, have frequently heard this concept. Psalm 95 is the pattern most frequently cited as *the* correct way. This psalm starts out with, "Come, let us sing for joy to the LORD; let us shout aloud to the Rock of our salvation. Let us come before him with thanksgiving and extol him with music and song" (Psalm 95:1-2). The idea put forth in this teaching is that we should begin with loud, exuberant praise. As the psalm progresses it brings us to the point of bowing down and kneeling (vs. 6). This all seems to be a very logical progression. However, nowhere does the Bible suggest that this is the once-and-for-all-time description of the proper progression in worship. We cannot simply take a section of Scripture and say that this is the way things must always be.

To show the fallacy of this kind of teaching, instead of Psalm 95 let's use Psalm 96 as our pattern. It starts out like this: "Sing to the Lord a new song; sing to the Lord all the earth" (Psalm 96:1). If we use this as our pattern then each time we gather for worship we must (a) sing a new song and (b) have the whole world singing with us. Obviously that idea is not going to work.

Having said all of that, allow me a moment to offer a practical positive thought. Although I certainly do not believe that there is an all-inclusive, always-correct pattern for worship, I have noticed a general guideline that can be helpful.

When people are gathering together for corporate worship their minds are frequently not all focused in the same direction. The things that happened on the way to church, the friend they just encountered in the foyer, their family concerns, and many other thoughts are all vying for their attention. Because of this, upbeat or lively songs can be a good way to start a service. This type of music has a way of capturing the people's attention more so than a quiet, meditative song. The goal is to focus widely-scattered thought patterns more quickly.

Please understand this is not an absolute. It is only a guideline. As you seek the Lord's guidance for a particular service you may find that you are led to start with something that is decidedly not upbeat or lively. It is better to pursue what you believe to be the leadership of the Holy Spirit than to follow a particular guideline.

The bottom line is that there is no one-size-fits-all answer. Pray for the Lord's guidance for each service. He will lead you.

Why, if two or more of us are seeking the heart of the Lord for a particular service, do we come up with completely different songs? Is one of us not hearing from God?

This question has caused a great deal of confusion and even division among those involved in leading praise and worship.

Let's start with the basics. First, you must have a pure heart in order to seek God (Psalm 66:18). This is not merely a suggestion or a good idea but an absolute necessity.

Beyond this, it is also necessary to have an understanding of how the Lord speaks through people. He will ordinarily work within your personality when speaking through you. Your past experience and present knowledge and circumstances will help determine how God works through you. Even Scripture shows this to be true. Matthew's account of Jesus' life differs in style from the writings of John but both are the inspired Word of God. If God actually spoke it, shouldn't they all sound alike? No. The Lord uses our individual vocabulary and understanding when speaking through us. He uses even the experiences that have shaped our lives when speaking His Word through us.

This is even true when seeking God for what songs to use during worship. A song that is ideal for one leader of worship in a given situation may not be appropriate for someone else's style of leading. This second worship leader may have a song better suited to him that will accomplish the same thing.

Each person has different musical tastes and will lean toward songs which speak personally to their heart. This means we need to be careful not to overdo our personal likes or dislikes and keep a balanced approach to song selection for a given time of worship. The converse of this is also true and needs to be understood: a worship leader is not expected to totally step out of his personality to the point of sacrificing his heart's drive in pursuing and worshipping God.

A good example of this is the way a church will take on, at least in a measure, the tastes and personality of its pastor. Leading worship is much the same. After a time, the music department and its functions will be generally influenced by the primary leader.

Several years ago, while still in the early stages of learning about worship leading, the man I was learning from gave me an "assignment." After prayer together with him and others involved in a specific worship service, I was to list the songs which I would use if I was leading. He did the same and then we compared lists. Out of lists that each contained about ten songs, there were three that were the same.

We discussed the lists and agreed that neither was more "correct" than the other, but each list was appropriate for the one who made it. Each would have accomplished the same thing. Our lists were different because we each had a distinct style and personality as a worship leader.

As a side note, I realized a few years later that even having only three songs out of ten that were the same was a very high percentage. I attribute it to my having learned so much from him: his style and personality had "rubbed off" on me.

Having differing song lists is not necessarily a sign that one of you is not hearing from the Lord. If all of the "basics" are in order and you both are seeking God from a pure heart, it simply comes down to the individualized method with which God chooses to interact with people. Do not panic or become uncertain... you are His sheep and His sheep hear His voice (John 10:27).

$\mathscr{D}$o you have some pointers for people on a praise team or choir ensemble leading worship to help them "focus." Please give some practical steps we can consider.

It is a good idea for those involved in the worship ministry to be prepared not just to play and sing but to worship the Lord. Their "focus" should be on God. In concrete terms there are numerous practical ideas that can be used.

Some people may find it worthwhile to simply take some time at home reading and studying the Bible. A few people have told me that they read scriptural promises of who they are in Jesus. Most people would admit that there are very few things that will help them focus more on the Lord than His Word.

Many individuals have mentioned that they find it helpful to arrive early at church and spend time in prayer. Often praise teams even spend concentrated time together praying before the service. This may take many forms including:

- praying for each other's needs and concerns.
- lifting up the musical aspect of the service, that you will be able to flow together as a unit and that God will be glorified through you.
- asking the Lord to demonstrate His grace throughout the service, because all of the musical preparations are of little value without the Holy Spirit's empowerment.
- interceding for the congregation to be prepared to meet with God and open to what He wants to do.

- praying for the pastor, that the Lord's Word will come forth powerfully and accurately, bringing conviction and encouragement.
- asking God to have His way in all that happens throughout the service.

Occasionally, worship ministries will have a brief teaching on some aspect of their ministry (servanthood, proper heart attitude toward God, etc.). A succinct but potent teaching right before the service can really help people focus.

There is no all-inclusive answer that is always right for every person in each situation. However, the fact that you recognize the importance of being focused means you're on the right track. Try these ideas and prayerfully consider other ideas of your own. In this way you can determine what works best in your situation.

Section 4

Leading Worship

What is the main thing to be concerned about in creating an atmosphere of worship at the beginning of the service?

Your main concern should be focusing the attention of the people on God. Unfortunately, there is no definitive way of doing this outlined in Scripture, but we can look at some practical considerations.

It is usually accurate to assume that not everyone is coming into the service with their hearts and minds focused on the Lord. People's thoughts are ordinarily running the full gamut of human emotions and cares. Some are joyful; some are tired; some may have encountered serious tragedy. All of these people need to be refocused toward God. For some, this will mean only a slight readjustment, but for others this could require a major shift.

How this is accomplished can vary as much as the people themselves. There is no easy answer that will work in every case. What is required is a worship leader that is sensitive to the Lord and the needs of the people.

Sometimes the best direction will be in fast, lively songs which guide people by word and music into a singleness of heart and mind. Other times, it may be more appropriate to start with a Scripture reading. Still other times, beginning with a majestic hymn may be the thing that is needed. Here are several other possibilities.

- Have the pastor welcome the people and share from his heart about the theme of the meeting.
- As the worship leader, do one song and then give a

short exhortation to interact with the people.

- After a medley of songs, have the people greet one another in the love of the Lord.
- After five minutes or so, have a responsive phrase or reading that people share with their neighbors.
- Do the announcements after one "gathering-in song." This way the announcements won't interrupt the flow of the service later.
- Have a pre-service prayer time starting 15 or 30 minutes before the service. This can greatly help people to be spiritually prepared for the actual service.

The main point is to change people's focus from themselves (or their circumstances) to God. Ask the Lord how to guide you for each particular service, and He will.

Why does it sometimes seem that worship just doesn't "get off the ground"?

Before answering the question directly it might be helpful to offer some preliminary thoughts. Worship might be "getting off the ground" and you simply don't realize it. A dear friend of mine shared that there have been times when one line of a song "hit me between the eyes." Because her heart was so touched by the truth of the words she was unable to continue singing the remainder of the song. Was she worshipping? Absolutely! But to the observer she might have seemed uninterested or not participative.

Sometimes God sovereignly works in people's hearts in the midst of praise and worship. This often causes different reactions in different people. Because of this it may well seem that the corporate response is not what was expected. However, it certainly does not mean that people are not involved.

With these thoughts as a foundation let's talk about worship that really doesn't "get off the ground." There can be many reasons for this. Some are very obvious such as interruptions and distractions or blatant unrepentance in the congregation. These usually leave little doubt as to why the worship is not going anywhere. However, there are occasionally other more subtle reasons.

One of the less obvious reasons is that none of us is yet totally adept at hearing and following the Lord's voice 100% of the time. Prayer, worship and studying His Word are all important keys in becoming better at this, but the fact is that we will not always perfectly follow His plan. Our ability to understand God's voice will grow and develop as we exercise that ability during meetings and in our everyday lives.

For us as worship leaders, this means that we will occasionally "miss it." Perhaps our preparation was based more on what we thought would work, rather than on honestly seeking the Lord's guidance. Or perhaps we were simply not listening as closely as we should have. Whatever the reason, we sometimes miss God's best.

There may be other reasons why we have "off" Sundays that we simply do not understand. It can happen to anyone at any time. Maybe the thing that God wanted to emphasize that particular day was the preaching of the Word. The worship may have been lackluster because the Lord wanted the sermon to "shine." The important thing here is how you handle it emotionally. If you decide that you are failing simply because you had an "off" day, then you are taking upon yourself unwarranted condemnation.

One key that can be very helpful in avoiding those worship-didn't-get-off-the-ground meetings is to learn to check people's faces and singing intensity every so often. In doing this you will begin to sense whether the people are with you in the worship. This may occasionally force you to move ahead to the next song or even to skip a few songs on your list and minister one which you had intended for later. Sometimes an exhortation that God is worthy regardless of how we feel may be in order. Perhaps a time of prayer is needed to release burdens that are keeping people from worshipping. In any case, you can take at least some of your cues from people's response.

Additionally, various activities that are not weekly events (baptisms, recognizing new members, communion, etc.) can cause additional time constraints and change people's focus. Keeping these things in mind will help keep you free from frustrations and disappointments concerning "good" and "bad" meetings.

Keep pressing ahead with God. As you learn and grow in Him, He will give you the necessary keys to do the job He desires for you to do.

ℳost churches today seem to follow a pattern of having praise and worship before the sermon. Why is this? Is it always correct to do it this way?

In a word, it is because of tradition. We long ago realized that praise and worship prepares people's hearts to hear God's Word. It "plows" up the "soil" of the hearts to receive the "seed" of the Word. It is so effective that it is now standard practice in many churches. It has, for all practical purposes, become a tradition.

Many independent/non-denominational churches tell me they do not have a set liturgy for their services. Yea, right! It usually goes something like this:

1) Praise and Worship
2) Announcements
3) Offering/Special Music
4) Sermon
5) Altar Call/Ministry
6) Dismissal

Many have said they do this to preserve order. I agree, order is necessary (1 Corinthians 14:40). Jesus would not even feed the five thousand until they were divided into groups of hundreds and fifties (Mark 6:40). We need order. But when we place our need for a set pattern above seeking God's plan for a service, we are limiting God's influence for that meeting.

As leaders, we should be in the habit of seeking the mind of the Lord for each service. Endeavoring to know what God wants to accomplish and how He wants to do it will help determine the order of the parts of that service. An obvious example of this is to have worship after a message about worship. Then we can actually do that which we heard about. Another idea is to follow a sermon about the miracles of God with a time of rejoicing. Or a message on the blessings of God can be followed by a time of testimonies about those blessings.

Beware of a potential major obstacle: people (even Christians) don't like change. An immediate drastic change from the norm can cause confusion and unrest. Change should be brought about slowly to assure the least number of "casualties."

Keep in mind that we as leaders are the ones who have propagated this tradition. We have conditioned people to expect music at the beginning of our services. So do not just throw out the opening music, but consider abbreviating it and having a more extended time of praise and worship later.

In using any of these ideas, be careful not to institute change just for the sake of change. In reality, that is no better than tradition for the sake of tradition. Instead, seek to be guided by the Holy Spirit into new and creative ideas for ordering your worship services.

*C*an a worship leader effectively lead God's people into a worship experience in 15-20 minutes?

Many churches must deal with very stringent time constraints. This can be because of multiple services on Sunday morning, television or radio broadcasts, being in a rented building with a strict schedule, etc. Unfortunately, each of these is a legitimate concern and must be reckoned with. Therefore, every segment of the service (worship, sermon, announcements, communion, special music, drama, offerings, etc.) must be carefully considered. If only 60 minutes are available, allowing 30 minutes or more for any one component is quite unlikely.

So if you have only 15-20 minutes for the praise and worship time, can it work? Yes.

Part of the reason that it sometimes does not is because the congregation has not yet fully understood that worship is not just a Sunday morning experience. I have heard it said that part of the reason worship does not occur in the pews is that it has not occurred during the rest of the week in life. If there has been no song in the heart for six days, there will not be one on the seventh.

The other side of the coin is this: when people realize that worship should be part of all areas of life, then the time constraints on Sunday morning make little difference. The corporate worship experience becomes a natural outgrowth of the worship that has been happening all week long. And limitation of time is insignificant.

These concepts should be taught from the pulpit, shared as exhortations during corporate worship and modeled by the leadership. The more thoroughly these ideas are instilled into the people, the more they will take root and bear fruit.

Yes, you can effectively lead worship in 15-20 minutes if the congregation truly understands worship as more than just singing songs on Sunday morning.

I am the worship leader at our church. Our services are more open and spontaneous. People are invited to share testimonies of what God is doing in their lives, prayer concerns, particularly meaningful Scripture passages, etc. On several occasions things have been shared which have impeded the flow of the service. Because most spontaneous sharings occur during the time of worship I feel I need to know what should be done to prevent this type of situation. Please help.

First, let me address a few words to those who may be unfamiliar with this type of service. A meeting of this nature is very common and even has biblical precedent (1 Corinthians 14:26). Allowing the opportunity to share tends to cause people to become more involved rather than simply sitting and observing. Unfortunately, there are also inherent drawbacks, such as the one mentioned above.

Sometimes people can be caught up in the emotion of what they are sharing. Perhaps it was a personal incident or something that happened to someone close to them. In any case, that same emotion may not be shared by others there. If the person shares for longer than necessary, the others have a tendency to begin to "tune-out."

Other times someone may share something that they think goes right along with what is happening in the service. However, that person's thinking may be on a different wavelength than everyone else's. If the sharer does not make the connection with what he is saying and what has been happening, everyone may be left feeling as though the train was just side-tracked.

Let me offer a few ideas that may help these situations.

Usually in this type of service the person goes to a microphone or is handed a microphone (talk-show host style). In this type of setting nearly anyone can walk up to a microphone at anytime and say anything that is on his mind. However, Hebrews 13:17 very clearly tells us that leaders keep watch over those under them. We cannot allow a domineering person to distract the attention of the congregation by consistently disrupting a meeting. When this type of thing happens we have abdicated our God-given role of leadership to someone who has no right to that role.

Being prepared beforehand to deal with a difficult situation is extremely helpful. Having a plan in coordination with the pastor (or whoever is in charge of the meeting) as to how to handle such scenarios will keep any one person from feeling alone in dealing with it.

Many churches that are involved in this type of service find it helpful to have people check with someone in leadership before sharing. In this manner a qualified person can discern beforehand whether what this individual wants to share is appropriate at a given time. The leader may give the okay, suggest waiting until later or veto the idea altogether. This way the words are screened or checked first, before the flow of the service is unnecessarily hindered.

Having a leader hold the microphone for the person sharing can be very helpful. In this way you have the ability to tactfully cut the person's monologue short and to wrap up what was shared if necessary.

Finally, this concept is not just a screening measure for the congregation. It will also help those who want to share to grow in their sensitivity. They will learn to be more accurate in their sense of timing and hearing God's voice. This will ultimately result in all of us being "built up until we all reach unity in the faith and in the knowledge of the Son of God and become mature, attaining to the whole measure of the fullness of Christ" (Ephesians 4:12-13).

During my years of leading worship, the most uncomfortable situations I have encountered have been either a technical problem (sound system, broken guitar string, etc.) or someone in the congregation playing an instrument. I have a degree in church music ministry, but these things were never discussed.

Let's look at these one at a time. What should you do when the microphones or sound system isn't working or when a guitar string breaks? These are a common but difficult problems. First, do all you can to try to fix the problem, but don't take too much time for this. Try not to let it become a distraction for you. As best you can, continue to worship the Lord and keep your eyes on Him.

Practically speaking, you might have a back-up plan for such situations. Your sound engineer should be able to handle the P.A. problems (i.e. switching microphone wires, etc.). A back-up guitar might be in order for a primary worship leader who is a guitarist. If a back-up guitar is unavailable, practice playing your guitar with a string missing. This will make you feel much less awkward if one breaks during a service. Often, these types of problems can be handled with a little pre-planning.

Now let's tackle the congregational-members-playing-musical-instruments problem.

Many churches tell those in the congregation who want to play any type of musical instrument during worship that they must audition for the music ministry. This keeps the instruments together for better interaction with one another.

In churches where this is not an absolute, the most common problem is percussion instruments (tambourines, etc.) being played (not very well) by people in the congregation. For best results, all percussion instruments should be played by people who are (1) rhythmically able to keep time and (2) positioned close to the drummer. A person who cannot keep time should not be allowed to continue to hinder the worship of others around them. If they pursue training and improve their ability, then work with them. If in the final analysis they just do not seem to have the necessary rhythm, pray and channel them into another area of service in the church.

(As a side note, one minister of music told me he will allow anyone in the church to play a tambourine as long as he can have it for five minutes prior to the service. He has a big roll of duct tape handy... Hey, a little creative planning ahead of time can be helpful.)

Secondly, because of sound delay and sound reflection, percussion players should be positioned in close proximity to the drummer (i.e., front row or close to the platform). This helps maintain a tight rhythmical unit. Someone sitting far away will be keeping time to a slightly delayed rhythm. Therefore they will be sending an even more delayed rhythm back toward the platform with their tambourine. Here again, it is vital to let the congregation know what is acceptable. This can be shared in written form (perhaps a new members packet) or from the pulpit. The important thing is to communicate in some form. They won't know if no one tells them.

If there is still a problem after this, it should be dealt with, preferably in private. Discuss with your pastor how it should be handled, but by all means, take care of the problem before it has a chance to grow and multiply.

I lead worship for a home group. How does this differ from leading worship on Sunday morning?

Home group meetings can sometimes be more difficult to lead in praise and worship than a regular church service. The obvious difference is the number of people. The dynamics of two hundred people singing is much different than ten or twelve in a home meeting. Generally in a larger corporate church service there are at least a couple of other instrumentalists working with you. In a home group setting it is usually just one person leading.

With you and ten other people staring at each other in close proximity the problem of self-consciousness can be greatly magnified. A lack of skill on the instrument you are playing can become more noticeable. This can produce more nervousness. All of these things can be overcome and, in time, make you a more accomplished worship leader.

When leading for a home meeting choose songs that work well for a smaller group. Songs that are more difficult should not be attempted, especially if these songs require a lot of additional instrumentation to make them work. The best idea is to keep the songs simple.

It should be understood that it is just as important to be spiritually and musically prepared for a home meeting as it is for a Sunday morning service. If it is viewed as less important, we are not being "faithful in the little things." Pray for God's direction for the meeting. Talk with the person leading the meeting. Be sensitive to the needs of the people. All of the things that would be normal for a larger setting are also appropriate for a home meeting.

Perhaps the first step is to realize the value of the worship leader. When we begin to recognize how important our role is, there will be an inner desire to take the time to prepare regardless of the size of the group. This preparation will cause a higher level of ministry to take place.

Section 5

Songs

Is it a good idea to explain or teach the meaning of lyrics of new songs during the service?

One of the keys to successful worship leading is for the worship leader to carefully examine and understand the lyrics of the songs that are used. It is extremely important for the leader to do this because those who are following rarely will.

Sometimes it is necessary to explain some of the words before teaching a song. People from various backgrounds may have a different understanding of the same words. To alleviate this problem a quick, simple explanation (an "Amplified Version" of the song) often helps immensely. Of course, many songs will need no explanation at all, but there will always be a few that do.

Obviously, your understanding the words is a prerequisite to an explanation. If you are uncertain about what a song is saying it is best to delay using it until you can clearly establish its meaning. This may seem obvious, but I have seen many people who do not follow this simple rule.

Next, try out your explanation verbally with a close friend. This is to be certain that you are actually clarifying (and not "mud-ifying") the meaning of the song.

In teaching new songs it is helpful if the lyrics are within the realm of experience and understanding of the congregation. Songs with a great deal of slang or hymns using medieval English will often not work well in certain congregations depending on the congregation's cultural orientation.

Many of the hymns written 200-300 years ago (or even

75 years ago) require a bit of study for us today to fully comprehend their meaning. This is not because the songs were poorly written but because the meanings of words and phrases have changed or the words have become outdated over the years. "Gladly for aye we adore Him" almost always needs an interpretation.

One of the important things to remember here is that music is an extremely potent vehicle. It can be used to lead or mislead, to guide into truth or into error. Through our music we have the power to properly teach Scripture and scriptural principles (Colossians 3:16; Ephesians 5:19), but sometimes we unknowingly use it to promote false concepts. Just as a great deal of secular music has taught immoral values to many people, our music must hold up God's standard and the truth of His Word. To make this reality the people must understand the lyrics. Therefore, at least occasionally, you will need to offer some explanation of those lyrics.

Several people in our church have labeled the modern praise and worship songs as "ungodly." They believe that the style of music is completely inappropriate for church. How do I handle these comments?

To date, I have been unable to find any indication from Scripture that God has a preference for a particular musical style. The fact is that music is simply a cultural vehicle and we should use it within the cultural setting where we find ourselves.

Some time ago I heard Bill Gaither speaking. He made a statement that really impacted me. Unfortunately I did not copy it verbatim, but the gist of what he said is this. "The gospel has always been the same since the beginning, but how it is packaged, the way that it is presented is always changing depending on the culture and society." He went on to say that he sometimes has difficulty relating to the type of music his son plays in church. However, he admitted that he could not deny the fact that his son is reaching people that he, Bill, will never be able to reach. We must begin to admit that even though we may prefer some styles of music over others, the others are not necessarily wrong. Music is simply a cultural vehicle.

Several years ago I encountered Dr. Judson Cornwall teaching at a worship conference. During one of his messages he addressed this concept of music and culture. Dr. Cornwall shared that he had on more than one occasion been to tribal regions in Africa to minister. For the music portions of their worship services they have what he refers to as "steel bands," any large metal object they can find to beat on to produce sound. Dr. Cornwall admitted that he preferred to have two aspirin before worshipping like that, but he could not deny the fact that the people were wholeheartedly giving themselves to God in worship. It was not his preferred style of music, but it was perfectly within the experience and understanding of that culture and society.

It is amazing to me to realize that missionaries in years gone by would take pipe organs into deepest, darkest Africa and compel the natives to worship in a style that was completely foreign to them. Is our Western style of music somehow more superior? Does our way of doing things somehow have more credibility with God because we have more Christians per capita? Obviously not. I am certain that the music David and others composed for the Psalms would sound extremely foreign to our ears.

The truth is that music is a cultural vehicle and must be seen as such. Martin Luther understood this when he adopted current tunes of his day and wrote good, theologically sound words for them. William Booth understood this when he wrote and performed songs (with his Salvation Army brass band) in the popular style of his day.

Did you know that J.S Bach — the father of Western church music — was once almost dismissed from his position in the church because people thought his harmonies and rhythms were too sensual? Bach!

Seeing music as a cultural vehicle does not give us license to use poor quality music. God is deserving of the very best quality we can offer. We must never compromise the highest standards of quality. However, even the high quality music of

J.S. Bach would probably not be readily accepted and whole-heartedly embraced by the people of rural Mongolia.

Several years ago I met a pastor from Trinidad. During our conversation he began talking about the steel drum, an instrument invented in his native land. The steel drum has long been a popular instrument in their musical style. This man went on to tell me how, many years prior, missionaries had come to their country and insisted that the steel drum was demonic. Many people stayed away from the church simply because of this pronouncement. Fortunately, today many churches throughout Trinidad (and many other countries as well) use the steel drum in their worship of God.

Today in our society there are numerous churches that use a style of music very much outside the cultural norm. Often what happens in these churches is that visitors cannot relate to the style of music and therefore go elsewhere. The truth of the Word of God may be there, but the music is too far removed from the experience and understanding of the people.

I am not suggesting that we throw out traditional hymns. Never! They are a vital part of our Christian heritage. I have seen many churches refuse to use hymns and I am convinced that this is very much to their detriment. However, to stay locked into a style of music that is 100-300 years old simply because this is the way we have always done it is just as detrimental.

Again, we must realize that music is a cultural issue. Why do the people in our society generally wear Western styles of clothing? Why do teachers in the church use modern English instead of the vernacular popular in the 1600s? Music, just like language and dress, is a cultural issue.

We must break out of being locked into a certain style of music and be willing to try new ideas and new ways of doing things. Remember, no particular musical style is more appropriate for the worship of God: it is strictly cultural preference.

What is musical sensitivity and how can we increase it?

As a young musician I sat listening to a well-known music group and wondered what made them so appealing. I realized later that it was not only because they used difficult musical techniques, but also because they had "musical sensitivity." They knew how to musically interpret each song to accurately portray the intent and emotions of the song.

As worship leaders we must fully understand that our songs are to be more than just a succession of musical notes tied to lyrics. It is essential that we begin to build our musical sensitivity and thereby to draw people into worship of God.

Many local church music teams seem to have a way of making various styles of music all sound alike. I have heard it described as putting the music through "the church blander." Whether it is a traditional hymn, an upbeat Jewish-style song, or a slow, meditative-type song, they all end up sounding very similar. This is not because of an intentional decision to make them sound the same; it is usually because of a lack of musical sensitivity as well as a need to update musical skills and talents.

The first practical step to improve is to realize that not all of the instruments available need to be played during every section of every song. If God has blessed you with numerous musicians, do not feel obligated to have them all play continuously. Be sensitive to the style and flow of the music, and choose instruments appropriate to the rhythm and style.

Consider this: Do symphony orchestra musicians play continuously on every piece? Of course not. Is it just because they are tired and need a break? No. Rather, the composer wrote the music in such a way that various emotions and concepts would be portrayed in different places by, at least in part, the use of different instruments.

We, too, need to apply this concept. God's power and might can be more accurately portrayed musically by a thundering bass guitar or a massive pipe organ than by a flute. Yet the flute would be a much better choice for a quiet, worshipful moment before the Lord.

Beyond instrumentation, we must also consider musical dynamics. Playing an entire song (not to mention several songs in a row) at the same tempo and decibel level can easily lead to boredom.

A carefully-planned crescendo can add life to an otherwise bland song. A properly-placed instrumental interlude will offer a time of contemplative individual worship. Singing the last line of a song several times (reprise, vamp, tag, etc.) can help drive home these final important words. Starting or ending a song with slower-than-normal tempo dramatically increases the impact of the words and music. Modulating to another key will musically lift and build a song. Dropping out all of the instruments while repeating a favorite chorus can have a dramatic impact on the singing.

One other practical suggestion is to continue to expose yourself to a variety of new music. There are many new praise and worship tapes with highly talented and innovative musicians on them. Listening to other players and singers will consistently help you improve your overall musical understanding. This will especially help yield ideas for growth in the area of musical sensitivity. There are no shortcuts in continuing to upgrade your ability, style and sensitivity. You have to keep listening to a variety of music.

All of these are simple musical tools that we can use. Some musical tools are very subtle but still quite effective. Others are more obvious, and, if overused, can lose their impact.

If you are not already utilizing these ideas, I encourage you to pray for an increased musical sensitivity. Then try some of these tools and trust God to show you how to best use them. Beyond the "natural" musical sensitivity of worldly musicians, we Christian musicians can tap into the real source of musical sensitivity. Ask the God of all creativity to show you new ways to musically express your worship.

I have been asked to add more variety to our music. Why is this necessary and how should I do it?

Why is it that God seems to stress singing new songs? Why does His word again and again entreat us to sing a new song to Him? (Psalm 33:3; 96:1; 144:9, Isaiah 42:10). Is it because God becomes tired of familiar words and music? I do not think so. I am convinced that when we see Him face to face and ask the reason, the Lord's response will be, "Children, it was not for My benefit but for yours."

Our Creator knows that we become bored very quickly in set forms and routines. Oft repeated words can soon become empty words. With enough repetition our songs soon take on the same depth of meaning as singing our favorite television or radio commercial jingle. We are not necessarily excited about the product, but the tune is catchy and the words are just a vehicle for us to ride across the music. If our worship has become like that, God has a prescription: sing a new song to the Lord. Not that this is a "catch-all, quick-fix" for our worship, but the freshness of new songs can bring new life to our times of worship.

There is a balance to this. I don't think that God would have us sing a song twice and forget it forever. The Bible has hundreds of songs recorded in it and we are encouraged to sing them. What I believe the Lord really wants is a freshness and a newness in our singing. Consistently. To do this on an ongoing basis can be a big job, but following are some simple, practical suggestions. Do not use them all next Sunday. Instead, slowly grow into them until you are comfortable with them and can use them effectively.

Men and women singing different parts. This can be done in different ways. Some songs lend themselves to descants or echoes (a type of "round" singing), and dividing the men and women can be effective on these. Almost all short choruses can work well to have women sing it once, then the men, and finally together.

Use different instrumentation. Some people have said this idea will not work for them because they only have one or two instruments. If you have one instrument, you can still vary your music by occasionally singing a cappella. With two instruments you can sometimes use just one, and later, just the other. With more instruments, you can do even more, but do not limit yourself by making it law that all instruments must play all the time.

Musical dynamics. I have heard it said that dynamics in our music are just as important as the notes we play. Music with no dynamics can be very blasé. Yet many churches seem to have two types of songs: loud and fast, or quiet and slow. Think about and evaluate the words and the music of your song and decide where a crescendo might be effective. Consider ways to break up those long quiet passages in your music.

Modulate to a different key. When you have done everything musically possible with a particular song and you want to go further with it, then modulating to a higher key can be extremely effective. Be careful with this, overuse can ruin its effectiveness. It can also put you in an uncomfortably high singing range. You should check the melody line of a particular song beforehand to know how high you can safely go.

Use various types of songs. Use songs in different keys and with different tempos. Use simple songs and complex songs. Use fast songs and slow songs.

Use soloists, duets and trio sets and even choirs. All of these can be very effective in adding variety even to old songs. Have a soloist sing the verses and have the congregation join in on the chorus. The choir (choirs are being integrated more and more into the praise and worship portion of the service) can sing a line and the congregation can repeat the line (antiphonal singing can be very effective).

Keep up with current praise and worship recording and trends. Visit your local bookstore occasionally and check for materials which you feel will work for you, your worship team and your church. When you get a new recording, listen for the songs which really minister to you personally or fit the type of praise and worship you are currently experiencing in your church. One important note here is to pay careful attention when looking for new songs. It is easy to overlook a great song because you are distracted while trying to listen.

The overall watchword for all of this is variety. But remember not to try substituting musical variety for real heart-felt worship. Instead, use your God-given imagination in adding variety to your music and you will see an exciting new dimension in your worship.

How much should the styles of music be mixed in one *worship service?*

It can be very healthy for a congregation to experience a variety of musical styles. However, trying to include many styles in any given service can be cumbersome or even confusing for people. If you want to include multiple styles in your church's music program, it is best to attempt it over a series of services rather than in a single meeting.

One church where I ministered recently utilizes several different music ensembles, each with a different style. The music pastor asks visitors not to judge the church from a single service. "Give us a month," he says, "and we'll show you a full array of musical styles." Indeed they do over a period of four Sundays, but certainly not all together in one service.

If you want to use several different styles of music for praise and worship, this approach seems to be better than trying to incorporate them all into one meeting.

As a worship leader, I get comments like, "We do too many fast songs" and "We do too many slow songs." Is there a balance?

The best overall solution is to get people to set aside their preferences and focus on the worship instead of the style. When Christians have God as the center of their attention, the style becomes far less important. Teaching can help cause this to happen, at least in some measure. However, to expect everyone to completely set aside all of their ideas and preferences is unrealistic.

I frequently tell worship leaders not to attempt to make everyone happy. You'll never do it. Everyone on the planet has an opinion on music whether they know anything about it or not. It is impossible to please everyone all the time. I have found that if I am hearing both sides of the argument in roughly equal numbers (i.e., "We do too many hymns," "We don't do enough hymns"; "We do too many slow songs," "We do too many fast songs") then we are probably pretty close to where we need to be for our church. You need to work at striking a balance that is right for your church's culture and area. Each church is different and what is "right" for another congregation may not be right for yours. You might even consider surveying the congregation (see Appendix).

Please don't ever totally ignore the comments. These are the people God is allowing you the privilege of leading in worship. Their thoughts on how you are doing are important.

If you hear several comments that seem one-sided, it might be good to discuss these with your pastor. Ask what he thinks about that particular topic. Maybe ask other people in church leadership how they feel about it. This can give you a much different perspective on the situation. It will also take it out of the realm of your opinion vs. the opinion of the vocal critic. If the pastor (and even other church leadership) agree or disagree with you, then there is a basis for changing what you're doing or leaving things as they are.

If you do decide that a change is in order, set a goal as to how to implement it. Ask your pastor to observe and offer feedback on how the changes are going. This gives you some accountability in bringing about the necessary alteration.

One other practical note: children (and non-reading adults) are much more comfortable with simpler songs. Songs with more complex words can be very difficult for these folks. Certainly you should not throw out the more difficult songs, but striking a balance can be helpful for many people.

What is the best way to introduce new songs to the congregation? Also, how frequently and how many?

There are some tried and proven ways to introduce new songs and also ways that have proven less than effective. One good way of introducing a new song is to use it as a special musical number prior to using it in worship. The week before its worship debut is a good time for this. Another possibility is to teach the song at the beginning of the service and then use it again later. This teaching method is especially helpful with songs that are more difficult. By using either of these ideas, the congregation is able to learn the song in a less-pressured atmosphere rather than attempting to learn it as they worship.

Teaching a brand-new song during a time of intimate worship is usually not a good idea. If the song is extremely simple, it may work, but generally, it can break the flow of worship.

When teaching new songs, there is a delicate balance to work toward when determining how many to teach. Because each congregation is different, there are no easy answers, but there are some general guidelines. If you teach too many new songs, the congregation will become frustrated trying to learn them; too few and your worship repertoire will become "stale."

The best gauge is congregational feedback. Because not everyone will be satisfied with what you do, it is best to try to strike a balance between the "too many" comments and those that say "not enough new songs." Practically speaking, many churches find that one song every two weeks (on average), or about 25 per year is very workable.

In forming a "master song list" what is the most useful way to structure it and what should it contain for each song?

There are nearly as many variations to a "master song list" as there are worship leaders. Listed below are some of the more popular components often used in conjunction with one another.

Songs listed alphabetically using title, first line of song (if different) and first line of chorus (if different). In listing the songs in this manner, a song could theoretically have as many as three listings. This is important because sometimes you may want to start a song at the chorus instead of the first verse.

Songs listed by key or key range. This is especially helpful for putting together medleys of songs. Using a key range instead of simply a single key can be very beneficial for modulations, medleys, etc.

Songs listed by tempo and time signature. Tempo is usually a generalized breakdown (i.e. fast, medium, slow). Again, this is important for medleys. Time signature is also necessary in making transitions easier. It is normally only listed on an index if the song is not in common time. Tempo and time signature are usually the most helpful when used in conjunction with the key listing.

Songs listed by theme. A listing of this type can be very useful in organizing a thematic service. For example, if you want to dwell on God's grace, a listing of songs having that theme would be extremely beneficial.

Scripture reference. This can be helpful in much the same way as the theme listing. It may also be beneficial to read the scriptural basis for a particular song before singing the song.

Corresponding reference number for transparencies and/or slides. Many churches that use transparencies or slides use reference numbers for each song. Each song is given a number (not unlike a hymnal) and is then listed on an alphabetical master list by title, first line and even first line of the chorus. In doing this each song can be listed up to three times on the master list. This can make the songs easier to find. In using this system, it is often helpful for the worship leader to have the reference number for each song.

These are the most popular song list components. Which ones to use and how they are organized will be determined by your particular situation.

I am confused over the whole issue of copyrights. As the worship leader at our church, what do I need to know about copyrights and the songs we use?

The easiest rule of thumb to remember is this: no copy of a copyrighted song may be made without permission from the copyright holder. The song itself should be thought of as a piece of property belonging to the copyright holder. Permission must be obtained to duplicate the song in any form (i.e. handwritten, photocopy, recording, etc.). To duplicate the song without permission is a violation of the law.

Copyright laws protect the rights of songwriters. These laws help assure songwriters that they will receive fair compensation for their works by those using them.

From your perspective, you need to be concerned about copyrights for the sake of your church. Making copies of songs, or even just lyrics (i.e. overhead transparencies, songsheets for your musicians, etc.) without permission, could potentially cause legal problems for your church. Technically, these copies would be illegal, and a lawsuit could be brought by the copyright holder. This is not a pleasant thought, but nevertheless, a very real possibility.

Researching the copyrights on the 300 or so songs in use by the average church can be a project of staggering proportions. Beyond this, paying each individual copyright holder an average of $10 per transparency can be far too costly for most churches.

Fortunately, today there is an organization, Christian

Copyright Licensing, Inc. (CCLI) that can help with copyrights and song usage. For one annual fee based on the size of your church, CCLI will allow you non-commercial use of the songs (within certain guidelines) for the period of one year. The initial fee is relatively inexpensive considering the number of songs and usage freedom received.

Avoiding copyright legal problems by joining CCLI[*] is important. However, for me the real issue is one of integrity. I must not break the law and take advantage of songwriters while leading people in worship. To do so would be a complete lack of concern for my brothers and sisters in Christ.

[*]For more information about CCLI call 1-800-234-2446.

Section 6

Relationship
to the Pastor and
the Congregation

Recently, we had a special service at our church. My pastor asked me to prepare for a "ministry and worship" time. During the service there was an intimate time of worship, and without really thinking about it, I knelt next to the pulpit and continued to sing. Then the pastor came over to me and said, "We are losing them. Get up and start leading." I did as he asked, but I must say my worship was somewhat quenched. When I got up, I looked around. Eyes were closed, hands were lifted although many were not singing.

My question is this: was I in error in my actions? And if so, where do you draw the line between being the worship leader and being a worshipper?

It is vital to establish and maintain good communication with your pastor. It may be worthwhile to have a consistent time of sharing about what happened in each service afterward. I would suggest that you ask your pastor what he meant when he said, "We are losing them. Get up and start leading." Is it possible that you misunderstood? Or is it possible that his idea of a "ministry and worship" time is different than your idea?

A good worship leader has sometimes had a broad base of exposure to various styles and depths of praise and worship. These may not match up with the pastor's understanding or his heart for a particular meeting. This is why asking for a clarification, especially in this instance, is important.

Here is an example of a better alternative in this specific situation. After the pastor's directive, it could have been helpful to instruct the other musicians and singers to continue in the time of worship. This would have given you the chance to briefly share with the pastor what you were sensing and your uneasiness in changing the current flow and direction. If you and the pastor have an understanding together about these times it is much easier, even on the spot, to check in with each other.

Another possible option for this situation is to simply continue the time of worship with a song that would flow with or further deepen the congregation's heart-response. In reality, even after you stood up you could have led into a song that would have carried on the same atmosphere.

An additional possibility is that your pastor could have made a mistake or been overwhelmed by the whole event. Just like you and me, pastors are still growing in the Lord.

To respond directly to your question, it is difficult to say, without hearing all view points, whether you were in error or not. It is correct that you as the worship leader are to be a worshipper as well as a leader. However, your pastor is still the one in charge in the congregation and in the service, and you must be willing to follow his leadership.

A good relationship with your pastor in which you communicate frequently will help alleviate lots of problems in the future.

My pastor doesn't give me much freedom in trying new ideas in worship. What can I do?

Three major things are important in this situation: prayer, communication and submission.

First, it is essential to pray both for yourself and for your pastor. Pray for yourself to be certain that you are going in the right direction (this is so easy to say and yet so hard to learn). Pray for your pastor that he might see all that God is wanting to do within your congregation.

Second, communicate. Beyond just the subject at hand, become his friend. Show care and concern that stretches past your professional relationship. With a solid foundation of communication at this level, discussion of new ideas and concepts will be much easier.

Third, decide in your heart that you will submit to your pastor. He may not agree with everything you suggest or all of your ideas, but if God has placed him in the role of leadership then you should esteem him fully in that role. Obviously, I am assuming that he is not in rebellion toward God and is attempting to follow the Lord's direction (even though you may not agree with all of his methods). The fact is that when your pastor knows that you are submitted to him, four things will happen:

1. He will find it easier to do his job as shepherd (you will be one less concern in his life).

2. He will not be afraid of you trying to usurp his authority (worship leaders starting their own

congregations over petty disputes seems to be an epidemic).

3. He will find it easier to hear from God (in his private devotional time and through you).

4. He will give you more freedom in your area of ministry (when he knows you're not going to try to "pull a fast one").

When our church's previous pastor left and another man filled the position, I pledged my complete loyalty to the new pastor. I voluntarily submitted to his authority. I did not do this to get something in return. I did it because it was the right thing to do. However, in taking this simple step I found immense freedom in my area of ministry. Because of my submissive attitude the pastor knew he could trust me completely.

The pastor of a church usually sees the congregation from an overall perspective, whereas the worship leader's vision may be more limited. Because of this, new and/or unusual ideas should not show up in the middle of the service on Sunday morning. Rather, take the time beforehand to talk with your pastor. Discuss the ramifications of your anticipated changes.

Remember: pray, communicate and submit. By doing these three things, you should see a new freedom in your area of ministry.

What do you do if the pastor says, "I want three hand-clapping songs and two slower, lead-into-prayer songs"?

I knew there would be at least one easy-to-answer question in this book. My answer is simple: I would do three hand-clapping songs and two slower, lead-into-prayer songs.

The writer of the book of Hebrews tells us, "Obey your leaders and submit to their authority" (Hebrews 13:17). The words "obey" and "submit" in this verse are not suggestions. They are commands. The pastor is in charge.

Although I may not always see eye-to-eye with him, he is still the boss. He is the one whom the Lord has seen fit to place as the overseer of the congregation. If I oppose his authority I am also opposing God's decision. I can think of few things that would be less productive than being in opposition to the Lord.

Because of this, as worship leaders, we should always have a servant attitude toward the pastor.

The relationship between the pastor and the worship leader in a church can be likened to a husband and wife. Just as a husband has authority over his wife, so does a pastor have authority over the worship leader. Whereas the wife (worship leader) has authority over the children (congregation), at the same time she must be in submission to her husband. Obviously this analogy (like nearly any analogy) has limitations. However, the truth is still there: as worship leaders we should obey and submit.

"Let me get this straight, pastor. You want us to do three hand-clapping songs and two slower, lead-into-prayer songs, is that right? No problem. We would be happy to."

I *desire to lead my church into a freedom of worship that they don't know exists. Our pastor is open to this but isn't sure where to start. Any ideas?*

Sit down with your pastor (and other church leadership) and discuss your ideas. Talk about the strengths and weaknesses of different styles of worship you have seen and various ideas you have encountered. Prayerfully consider each of these and how they would impact your congregation. Which things would be right and relevant for your church and which would not?

In considering any changes, you should develop a plan and a tentative time line for implementing those changes. What tangible results do you expect to see in six months? One year?

In your planning, keep in mind the music director who had a powerful experience in worship at a renewal conference. In his enthusiasm he tried to introduce everything he had seen and heard at the conference to his congregation on the following Sunday. It was not a very pleasant experience, to say the least. Your congregation will need time to adjust to the changes that you are introducing.

A good first step is solid biblical teaching on worship. We too often take more cues about what is acceptable worship from our society than from the Bible. A clear understanding from Scripture about what worship is, why we worship and how we worship can be extremely beneficial in moving people forward in true worship.

I highly recommend that you not make any changes for a couple of months but simply inform the congregation that some modifications are being considered. Little by little let the people know what sort of changes are coming. This will prepare them for the changes and minimize fallout.

When you actually start making the changes be very cautious and go very slowly. Perhaps you will decide that in twelve months your church will regularly be singing a couple of contemporary praise and worship songs during the Sunday service(s). After the first year, maybe occasionally inviting people to raise their hands to the Lord would be a good goal.

Throughout the entire process consistently check in with the pastor and other leadership of the church to get their perspective on how the people are responding. Remember to take it slow so as not to overwhelm the congregation. People do not like change. Some refuse to change even when a solid scriptural basis is shared.

In offering these suggestions I am assuming that your congregation really loves God and is desiring to move forward in His kingdom with their lives. If this is true then these ideas will help you move forward.

I've found that if I'm harboring some resentments or have a problem with other believers, I am often hindered from fully worshipping. Any comments?

?

Your relationships with your brothers and sisters in the Lord will affect your worship. Most people never even think about this, but it's true. Let me explain.

"So then you are no longer strangers and aliens, but you are fellow citizens with the saints, and are of God's household, having been built upon the foundation of the apostles and prophets, Christ Jesus Himself being the corner stone, in whom the whole building, being fitted together is growing into a holy temple in the Lord; in whom you also are being built together into a dwelling of God in the Spirit" (Ephesians 2:19-22).

This says that the Lord is building His people together into a "holy temple." He is unifying us into "a dwelling of God." Most of us understand this idea but few recognize the purpose for this building.

"You also, as living stones, are being built up as a spiritual house for a holy priesthood, to offer up spiritual sacrifices acceptable to God through Jesus Christ" (1 Peter 2:5). The building is to be a place of spiritual sacrifices. It is the central place of our praise and worship. So what happens when this building is not constructed well? The spiritual sacrifices are lacking; they are not all that they should be.

However, the normal tendency for us when worship seems to fall flat is, "Well, I guess the worship leader didn't hear from God today," or, "The musicians didn't practice enough." But often, what we really need to do is look at our relationships with our brothers and sisters to see if that is the problem.

Consider the man who comes to a worship service and looks scornfully on his younger brother in Christ because of hair length and clothing styles. The younger man may have a strong Christian walk, but it doesn't make any difference since he looks weird. Simply based on appearance, the older brother has decided to have no relationship with him. In doing so, the walls of the building are weakened.

Or how about this scenario: there is a woman in your church who regularly tells everyone who will listen about "the exciting things the Lord is showing her." But as far as you are concerned, she's simply an annoyance. Because of this, you have decided not to have anything to do with this sister. No matter that she is a child of God, the fact is she is not "your type of person."

Have you ever done this? If so, how do you think God views this type of action?

"Do you not know that you (plural) are a temple of God, and that the Spirit of God dwells in you? If any man destroys the temple of God, God will destroy him, for the temple of God is holy, and that is what you (plural) are" (1 Corinthians 3:16, 17).

The word "destroys" here literally means "to mar" or "to damage." In Bible times, if anyone were to damage the walls of the temple they would have been killed. There was no question about it — damaging the walls of the temple in any way was absolutely forbidden. Yet we damage the walls of God's temple every time we come together with strained or severed relationships. We are defiling the dwelling of God.

A few weak stones in the walls won't cause problems, but stones that are not properly fitted together, whose relationships are not in order, will make the wall very weak. Then the spiritual sacrifices will be lacking.

Your attitudes toward your brothers and sisters in Christ can affect the corporate worship. If your relationships with fellow-believers are not all that God wants them to be, determine in your heart to make them a high priority in your life. When you do this, you will see a difference in your worship life.

I understand the pastor's role within a given church, but what is the proper relationship between a worship leader and congregation?

?

First, the worship leader should be seen as a leader in the congregation. Of course this is not on the same level as the senior pastor. Nevertheless, it is still a leadership position. Many congregations view this person as an assistant pastor.

The worship leader should be officially set in place (1 Chronicles 16:4-7; 25:1). His authority should be defined, recognized and submitted to.

The worship leader, in turn, should be totally committed to leading the people in worship in spirit and truth (John 4:23). His heart should be to encourage and help this group of believers to move on in the area of worship. A primary motivation should be to see the people come into their high calling in God, using praise and worship as one of the vehicles to do this.

The worship leader's interaction with the people should be handled carefully. Although a loving, caring relationship should be cherished, too many compliments can prove difficult to handle. Even a humble person can have his ego inflated by too much praise. The worship leader must learn to allow honor to pass through him and on to God.

On the other hand, opposition from congregational members can be very destructive. Opposition usually comes in the form of stylistic disagreements. Specifically, someone doesn't like the way certain things are done (i.e. "It was too loud today," or "We never sing my favorite song, 'Drop-kick Me Jesus Over the Goal-posts of Life,'" etc.). Unfortunately, even though these items are usually based solely on opinion, they can still be very divisive. The worship leader should hear the person out and consider what he is saying. If the problem is serious enough, perhaps the pastor will need to mediate. In any event, don't let a minority voice of opposition harm your relationship with the congregation.

Always maintain love-motivated relationships. In doing this you will be well on your way to finding the ideal relationship God has for you and your congregation.

ow much responsibility do those leading in praise and worship have to lead worship in a way that is in sync with the members of the congregation? For example, there have been times when we have raised our hands during worship and many in the congregation look at us as though we were aliens.

The primary purpose of leaders is not necessarily to be popular, but to lead. Sometimes this means taking people beyond their comfort zones and into areas where they have never been before.

There is a scriptural precedent for this concept. King David did not take a survey about the acceptability of dancing in praise to God before embarking on such an outrageous act (2 Samuel 6:14, 15). He simply did it. The people saw his obvious love for the Lord. For the dedication of the temple, Solomon knelt in prayer on an elevated platform (2 Chronicles 6:12, 13). It seems obvious that the purpose of the platform was not so Solomon could be a few feet closer to God. It was so the people could see him kneeling in prayer. He wanted to be an example of a leader who sought God. Today, also, Christians need examples of true worship being expressed to the Lord.

Several years ago there was a young woman in our church whose countenance and mannerisms during worship expressed an undeniable love for God. Her adoration for her Savior was extremely obvious. Knowing that she had a good singing voice, I invited her to become a part of our music ministry. I explained that more than needing her voice, I wanted the congregation to see what it's like to be passionately in love with God.

Good examples — role models — can play an important part in people understanding various aspects of life. This is true also for praise and worship. If people look at you strangely when you raise your hands, just keep it up. Some day, because of your example, they too may influence others to express worship to the Lord.

How do you instruct and/or encourage members of the congregation to prepare for worship?

The best way is through consistent teaching and exhortation. This may be by way of the sermon or just little thoughts shared by the pastor or worship leader during the service.

Generally, people see worship as something for Sunday morning. Until they understand that worship should permeate all of life they will always struggle with the corporate worship experience.

Practically speaking, you can share Bible passages regarding praising and worshipping God all day long. Scriptures such as Psalm 34:1, Psalm 113:3 and Hebrews 13:15, all tell us that praise is to be an everyday part of life. It is not reserved for just Sunday morning. Offer thoughts on people in the Bible who actually praised God in their everyday existence. You could talk about David in Psalm 27:4-6 or Paul and Silas in jail (Acts 16:25).

Another suggestion is to relate ideas from our culture that might help people grasp this concept. "Would you go to meet with the president of the United States without making some preparation? How much more should we prepare to meet with the President of presidents, the King of kings and the Lord of lords?"

The important thing in all of this is to be persistent. Don't have the attitude of, "We told them once, what's their problem?" Other people are just like you. They have bad days. They get spiritual amnesia. They don't consistently bolster their walk with the Lord. Because of this we all need consistent reminders to keep pursuing the things of God. "But encourage one another daily… so that none of you may be hardened by sin's deceitfulness" (Hebrews 3:13).

All of these ideas can help motivate people to understand that their own personal preparation will play a vital role in the corporate experience of worship.

Section 7

The Music/Worship Team

When starting a new worship team in a small church, what would be the first instruments to start with and which ones would you add next?

?

When starting a new worship team, it is usually best to start with foundational instruments such as a keyboard or guitar. These instruments can incorporate all three basic components of music: melody, harmony and rhythm. Other instruments can enhance one or two of these areas but not all three.

Before you begin to build on this foundation, be certain that the foundation is solid. Your key instrumentalist(s) should be well-versed in both the musical and spiritual aspects of worship and worship leading. This will become of primary importance as your team begins to grow. If your main instrumentalist(s) is lacking in either area then, quite probably, the entire team may eventually be lacking also. As you do begin to add other instrumentalists it is important to look for the same musical and spiritual qualities in them also.

The next instruments to add would be additional keyboard, guitar, bass and drums. These will fill out your rhythm band and give a solid foundation to whatever you want to accomplish musically.

Beyond this, the instruments that you add will be determined by the sound for which you are looking. This, in turn, will be determined by the people to whom you are ministering. People raised on country music may not relate well to a "jazz" sound or a pipe organ. So be practical in adding instruments and don't necessarily just grab the first musician that comes along. Build slowly with deliberate planning for where you are going. Be sure to take into consideration such practical aspects as space and sound system limitations.

I lead worship in a very small congregation. We only have a few musicians and cannot seem to produce the full musical sound which is so popular in today's praise and worship music. Any advice?

To begin with, let me address some preliminary issues before answering your actual question. First, simply because something is popular (i.e. "full" sounding music) doesn't mean it is *the* goal for which you should strive. Many times very light accompaniment (or no accompaniment at all) is preferable to a large sound. Reverent times of intimate communion with the Lord are usually better served with very little (and very sensitive) instrumentation, than with overwhelming sound.

Second, it should be noted that worship does not equal music. This means music of any kind, whether loud or soft, full or slight. Worship, true worship, comes from the heart. Though musical accompaniment may affect our emotional response, we can, without question, have a satisfying, God-pleasing time of worship with little or no musical accompaniment.

Both of these first two concepts should be taught to our musicians and our congregations. We must all understand that music does not necessarily "make" the worship. Music is simply a vehicle by which we may convey our worship.

With this foundation, there are some practical steps you can take to achieve the goal mentioned in your question. First, it is vital in these formative stages of your worship ministry, that your worship team begins to utilize musical sensitivity and dynamics. They must fully understand the concept that every instrument should not be played constantly at full volume.

You did not mention the exact instruments you have available, but let's try some specific examples. If you had a piano, guitar and flute, it would be appropriate for all the instruments to play at full volume altogether during an upbeat, joyful song. When using a more contemplative song, you might do better to have just the piano and flute. Still other times, such as an intimate love song to the Lord, sensitive finger-picking by the guitarist, with no one else accompanying, might be in order. By using your instruments sensitively you can enhance the times you achieve your full sound. Because the instruments are not all playing all the time, when they do all play, it will sound much more full.

Second, you can pray for the specific instruments which you would like to add. List those instruments which you most desire to have available and ask your other musicians, your pastor, and even the congregation to pray for the Lord to bring them in. Be specific in your requests and also ask for musicians who are talented and committed to God.

One of your initial main considerations for additional instruments might be an electronic keyboard. Today many quality electronic keyboards are relatively inexpensive. By utilizing one of these versatile instruments, you can add a variety of instrumental sounds which you might otherwise never have the opportunity to use in your music. The only caution is that to play an electronic keyboard to its fullest potential requires a great deal of musical sensitivity, much more than any other instrument.

When you do begin adding musicians to your praise band, be careful to use a great deal of discretion. The heart attitude of the musician is more important than his musical ability. It is not usually a good idea to add several musicians at once either. This can hinder the musical "flow" which your present musicians have already developed with one another.

Using these simple ideas over the long term you should be able to achieve the full sound you desire.

What type of guidelines do you recommend for the members of our worship team?

I highly recommend having some type of written guidelines for the music ministry of every church. Many problems could easily be alleviated with proper communication. Written guidelines can help immensely in this regard.

I suggest having guidelines in two categories. The first section would be what type of qualifications you are looking for in new team members. This could include things like:

membership at your church — Emphasize that someone passing through or just checking out the church is not eligible to be a part of the music ministry.

spiritual maturity — Although an exact definition for this may be difficult, it is certainly important.

musical ability — What level of expertise are you expecting?

free time — Having enough time to commit to the music ministry may seem obvious but is often not considered.

support of family — Having the support of the spouse, older children or parents can be important.

The second section would include your expectations of people once they are a part of the music ministry. This might include:

probationary period — This can help the person learn to flow with the rest of the team and give you a chance to work carefully with them in a non-ministry situation.

rehearsal attendance — Do they need to attend every rehearsal? Is punctuality a necessity?

ministry — Are they expected to minister at every regularly scheduled service? If not, how often? What about special services?

spiritual preparation for ministry — Music is not the first priority, worship is. Emphasize this early and often so people understand.

musical excellence — Do you expect them to practice the songs on their own? What about improving their musical skills (i.e., lessons)?

spiritual growth — A commitment to continued maturing in their Christian walk should be a high priority.

appropriate dress — What do you consider acceptable attire for ministry? Does it vary depending on the meeting? Does weather make a difference?

All of these things should be carefully considered and addressed. These ideas are certainly not meant to be an all-inclusive list. They are simply thought-starters. There may be other considerations depending on your situation. You may want to include your pastor or other church leadership in the process of determining what guidelines are right for your church.

If you are just starting a worship ministry at your church implementing guidelines right from the beginning is best. However, if you already have an existing music ministry, it would probably be best not to hand out a list of new guidelines at a rehearsal without any prior warning. I suggest that you discuss the guideline idea with your pastor first. With his approval, inform those involved in the music ministry that you are considering implementing guidelines for everyone involved. After they have had time to think about this concept (6-8 weeks) let them know that you are working on actually formulating guidelines. Again, after they have had time to contemplate that announcement (6-8 weeks) share a couple of the guidelines you are considering. Give them time to recognize the importance of these ideas (yup, you guessed it, 6-8 weeks), before actually handing out the final guidelines. This may seem like a very slow, drawn-out process but it will minimize fall-out over the long haul. People do not like change and the more you can prepare them for any changes the fewer problems you will encounter.

Clear communication in the form of written expectations will help strengthen your church's music ministry.

*I*n our church there is a lady who obviously loves God with all her heart and worships Him. She has asked about becoming one of the music ministry singers but she does not sing very well. I'm not certain how to handle this.

As a general rule it is necessary for a person to have some level of proficiency in the task they are desiring to perform. This is true in nearly any area of life — brick laying, cooking, and, yes, music ministry. This seems obvious. The difficult part is determining exactly what level of proficiency is adequate for the situation.

Some churches are comfortable with taking someone not very skilled and having them improve as they participate. This is a sort of learn-as-you-do-it approach, almost an apprenticeship concept. These churches frequently use the numerous "make a joyful noise" passages as their basis. Other churches have very strict criteria that demand those involved be at an extremely high level of musical proficiency. Churches from this school of thought would point to Psalm 33:3 as their guide: "play skillfully." And of course there are many churches that position themselves somewhere in between these two extremes. So what's the right answer?

Unfortunately, Scripture does not give clear instructions on the correct answer to this question. The temple musicians listed in 1 Chronicles 25 were all "trained and skilled in music" (1 Chronicles 25:7). However, it goes on to say that the "young and old alike, teacher as well as student, cast lots for their duties" (1 Chronicles 25:8). Although they all had at least some level of skill, apparently there was no forethought given to putting the less-skilled musicians with the more accomplished ones. No distinction seems to have been made.

Since the Bible does not give a clear indication in one direction or the other, then it seems safe to assume that either could be correct depending on the situation and circumstances. A smaller church may find it necessary to recruit people of lower skill levels, simply because that is what is available. Larger churches, with more people to pick from, may decide to raise the standard.

The important point in all of this is to decide what is right for your church. Maybe the apprenticeship concept will work well for your situation, and after prayerfully considering it, you decide it is right for your congregation. Great. Do it with all your might. However, in following that course, don't begrudge another church's decision to follow a different path. Decide what is right for your setting and your people and then do it.

One final practical thought: if the person's singing ability is so poor it would be distracting you might be able to offer another part of the worship ministry as a place of service. Things like running overhead projectors or organizing the worship ministry music can be real acts of service and worship.

Formulate carefully thought-out and clear guidelines of what type of criteria will be used to decide who does (or does not) participate in the music ministry. Share these with those who are interested. This will save you from needing to make up the rules as you go along.

*S*ome of the musicians on our worship team have expressed a desire to face away from the congregation and toward the front wall when we are leading worship. They feel that since we are really "ministering to God" that this would be appropriate. Also, they don't want to get caught up in a feeling of pride from being "up front." What should I do?

First, leading worship is not strictly God-oriented. The very name "worship leader" implies that someone is being led. It's not God that we're leading. It's the people. An effective worship leader is not just a good singer or instrumentalist, but, more importantly, is an example of a worshipper.

In 2 Samuel 6 the Ark of the Covenant was being brought back to Israel. King David could have waited until it arrived or simply thanked God within the confines of his home. But instead he joined the procession and he danced before the Lord "with all his might." Not only was David worshipping God, but he was — as a leader — being an example of how to worship God.

King Solomon also understood this principle. At the dedication of the temple as recorded in 2 Chronicles, Solomon had a large platform erected. In 2 Chronicles 6:13 it says that he "knelt on his knees in the presence of all the assembly of Israel, and spread out his hands toward heaven." Solomon wasn't trying to impress anyone — he just wanted the people to know that the leadership that was over them was sold out to the Lord.

Having said all this, falling into pride is a legitimate concern. With the team concept which you are using, watching out for one another is helpful. Talk regularly about what you are doing and why you are doing it. This not only helps alleviate temptations to become prideful but also builds strong relationships.

Teach these concepts to your worship team (or have your pastor do it). These ideas will build within them a strong foundation for being examples in worship.

It seems that every church I visit has the musicians arranged differently on the platform. Are there any guidelines as to what is best?

Many churches ask about practical ideas in platform arrangements of musicians and singers. Obviously, it is impossible to cover every situation in every church because of the many variables in congregation size, physical space limitations, etc. But by carefully considering the following suggestions you will hopefully find some ideas that are applicable to your situation. These will be especially helpful for considering future platform positioning and for those involved in new building plans.

Worship Leader's Proximity to the Congregation

Some churches have a platform which is quite far removed from the congregational seating either by height or by horizontal distance. Because a good worship leader will often take his cues from the response of the people, too much distance can hinder this vital interaction. Sometimes, worship leaders prefer to have a large distance between them and the people, but this is usually because they feel that the distance somehow gives them more credibility or authority (i.e. "I am the leader"). However, if a person is committed to leading people in worship (as opposed to just putting on a show or being "up in front"), he should seek the proper balance concerning proximity. For extremely large congregations this may be impractical, but for most churches, the worship leader can be easily positioned close to the congregation. The closer the placement of the primary worship leader or team to the congregation, the better the interaction.

The Rhythm Band

The rhythm band is usually considered the musical core of a church's worship team. Sometimes it makes up the entire worship team. A rhythm band consists of piano (and/or electronic keyboard), guitar(s), bass and drums. These are the basic instruments that carry the rhythm and play the harmony on which the melody is built. Other instruments (flute, violin, oboe, harp, etc.) are considered solo instruments and are less foundational (musically speaking). Therefore, they aren't considered a part of the rhythm band.

It is important that the members of the rhythm band be placed close together. There is a tight rhythmic interaction which takes place during services and rehearsals. Without these musicians being in close proximity to one another, there can be real problems with tempos, rhythms, chord progressions, and basic communication.

Many churches have an organ on one side of their platform and a piano on the other side. Some churches even put drums on the opposite side of other percussion instruments (congas, timpani, etc.). Although aesthetically such an arrangement looks very nice, musically, it is ineffective. These key foundational instrumentalists should be positioned near each other to allow them the musical interplay which they need (i.e. the bass player can match some of the drummer's kick drum patterns, etc.).

Worship Leader's Sight Line to Key Musicians

Just as the rhythm band members must have interaction with one another, the worship leader must be able to interact with at least certain key musicians. This is, of course, assuming that the worship leader is not one of the rhythm band members. If he is, then the necessary interaction is simple. If, however, the worship leader is not a rhythm band instrumentalist, then certain arrangements are vital.

The most significant of these is the sight line to both the drummer and the lead accompaniment instrumentalist (usually piano). The worship leader must be able to indicate desired tempo changes to the drummer at any time. In the same way he must be able to communicate key changes or song changes, etc., with the main accompaniment instrumentalist. Without this communication, his leadership is greatly hindered. If the worship leader has an unobstructed view to these two primary musicians, then communication is much easier. Simple hand signals to indicate tempo changes, modulations, song endings, etc., are very effective if the primary players are within easy view.

Vocalists

The primary vocalists are usually as follows:
- worship leader singing melody
- 2 or 3 "natural ear" harmony singers
- an additional melody singer, especially if the worship leader does a lot of embellishment work or "improv."

These primary vocalists should be positioned close to each other in the same way as the rhythm band. This will help them in hearing one another and avoiding clashing harmonies. If monitors are used, this can help immensely, especially if the vocalists can be given a more vocal-oriented monitor mix. If possible, each of these primary vocalists should have his/her own microphone to help obtain the proper levels in the overall sound (house p.a.) mix.

If a choir is being utilized, they can be positioned off to the side as long as they can hear (preferably through monitors) the instruments and other vocals. Many churches making a transition to praise and worship simply leave their choirs where they have always been positioned.

Other Instrumentalists

Additional instrumentalists outside of the rhythm band need to be handled carefully. They can be placed away from the rhythm band, (with proper monitors) although it is helpful to have them as close as possible. Individual miking of these instruments is usually not necessary, although occasionally a solo by a certain instrument may be miked. Additionally, separate your instruments according to other proven arrangements like those of symphonic orchestras or larger churches who are already utilizing many instruments.

Visual Projection Equipment

Many churches use overhead transparencies, slides or computer projection equipment to project song lyrics onto a screen or wall for the congregation to sing. Although under the best circumstances these are very effective, sometimes there are problems. Placement of the projector can be crucial.

Two major considerations are important:

1. The words should be easily viewed by the entire congregation (sometimes two projectors are needed: one on each side of the room). Very often, without two projectors,

many of the people in attendance will be unable to fully participate.

2. The projector(s) should not interfere with the musicians.

Some churches have the projector positioned so that it actually shines in the eyes of the musicians. This can be a real problem if they are trying to read music. There is also a potential for blocking the sight lines between musicians. Make sure the musicians communicate with the projectionist(s) to avoid any problems.

In all of these things please keep in mind that Scripture does not give us any absolutes about platform arrangements. The practical suggestions offered here come from years of worship leading experience. Hopefully, they will benefit you and your church.

Do all praise and worship teams attract "unstable" people or is our church the only one? Help!

The book of 1 Samuel tells about the people who gathered around David before he became king. "All those who were in distress or in debt or discontented gathered around him, and he became their leader" (1 Samuel 22:2). I have always thought that this description sounds a lot like most church music ministries.

Musicians are frequently a bit flighty (I've been told that musicians are temperamental: half temper and half mental!). They are often the more creative, visionary type of person. Generally, the better the musician is, the more this is true.

That's the bad news. The good news is that David's in-debt, in-distress, discontented folks became a powerful army under the leadership of a true worshipper. The same can happen in any worship ministry today. Musicians can be some of the most committed and compassionate people in the church. Please understand that it may take a fair amount of effort on your part to get them to that point, but it's worth the effort.

Love them. Care for them. Show them your heart and your commitment to the church and the worship ministry. These things will go a long way toward helping them understand their role.

Along with the demonstration of what you're looking for, teach them. Frequent communication about how vital their role is will make it more real in their minds, and therefore in their lives.

In addition to this, having carefully thought-out guidelines for the worship ministry will help immensely. Using this concept, the people all know ahead of time what is expected and what will be required of them.

Please realize that heaven is still in the future. You will not find perfection before you arrive there. However, with some care and understanding, leading a worship ministry — even one full of slightly off-kilter musicians — can be extremely fulfilling.

ow do you deal with the "glitter attraction" of worship ministry? People seem to be attracted to our worship team for the wrong reasons.

?

This can indeed be a problem with any type of up-front ministry. People sometimes want to be a part of the worship ministry because they want to be seen. Obviously this is a misguided motivation.

The best way I have found to deal with this is through the use of guidelines for the worship ministry. When people recognize the commitment level that is required, they will usually have second thoughts about whether or not this is really what they want to do.

One specific part of our guidelines is a probationary period for anyone joining the music ministry. For three months they are required to come to our rehearsals, but they are not allowed to minister with us for our services. There are really two reasons for this. First, this gives them time to learn the music and learn to flow with us as a musical group. The other reason is really for a heart check. It is fairly safe to assume that if they are willing to make the commitment of practicing with us each week for three months, that they are not just wanting to be seen up in front. Obviously, this is not always a guarantee, but it is generally a good indicator of a proper heart attitude.

Additionally, sharing your heart about the real purpose of the music ministry can be a big help. When potential worship team candidates understand that our real role is that of a servant, it can cause them to rethink their motivation in wanting to be a part of that ministry.

There will always be the "glitter" attraction to the music ministry, but these ideas can help keep those who ultimately become involved for the wrong reasons to a minimum.

How should I deal with problems within our worship team?

There are numerous types of "problems" which may be encountered in your situation. I will attempt to address a few of them.

The first priority in dealing with any type of problem is to avoid having the problem in the first place. This may seem obvious, but many of us often overlook the obvious. Specifically, having guidelines for the members of your team will give parameters within which they are expected to function. Without written guidelines they don't know what is and is not acceptable.

When you do encounter problems, it is very important to address them as soon as possible. Although none of us enjoys confrontation, it is important not to allow the problems time to grow and fester. For example, if there is a continual problem with tardiness by one or more individuals within the group it should be addressed as soon as it is obvious. If you let it continue it will only get worse.

Sometimes a competitive spirit can creep in. This is especially true among musicians, and even Christian musicians. One person will begin to have an "I'm better than you" attitude, and soon this can permeate the entire group. Here again, prompt action is essential. First, be careful to check your heart and motivation. Then privately discuss the problem with the person. Let them know what you have observed and what change you would like to see. If change does not occur and a further confrontation is necessary, consider disciplinary action (i.e. "probation," temporary or permanent dismissal from the team, etc.).

Another common problem is lack of commitment (i.e. missing practices, poor attitude, not learning songs, etc.). There can be several reasons for this including: increasing home and/or work pressures, spiritual laziness, etc. The root of the problem should be determined first. If it is a temporary dilemma (i.e. increased workload during a particular time of year) this should be dealt with in a less drastic way. Maybe a temporary leave of absence from the team would be in order. Other reasons may require different solutions.

In all of these situations, the problem must be dealt with as soon as possible. An immediate private loving confrontation is the best way to keep it from becoming worse.

How do you combat, "God gave me this gift, I don't need to practice"? They say it in all honesty.

This is an unfortunate but not uncommon scenario. Let me attempt to offer some practical ideas.

In essence everything we have is from God. Our abilities and talents, financial blessings, family and more are all gifts from the Lord. Does this mean I never need to do anything with any of these. Absolutely not.

When my wife and I bought our home, God gave us a lawn. If we never do anything with that lawn, what will happen to it? Also, God gave us children (Psalm 127:3). What would happen if we were to never do anything with those children. We have an obligation to be good stewards of the gifts the Lord has given (Matthew 25:14-30).

For musicians this may mean further lessons and study to improve abilities and understanding. Perhaps a course on music theory at a local junior college would be in order. Possibly private lessons for instrument or voice would be helpful.

At the very least regular, consistent practice is essential. Without this, your musical abilities will stagnate.

God may have given the gift but it is up to us to be faithful stewards of those gifts.

How do you get musicians of very differing talent levels to work together?

This can be tricky. Often the more talented musicians can have an attitude of superiority while the less talented may feel intimidated. Obviously this is not very conducive to a good working relationship. The best solution I have found is to endeavor to build strong relationships among those involved.

There is a dimension of competitiveness built in to music performance. Through years of lessons and training we are taught to try to be the best. Unfortunately, this attitude is very prevalent among Christian musicians and even those involved in worship ministry.

Building solid relationships among the musicians can help alleviate this. The reason is simple. Friends — true friends —don't want to compete against one another in any negative sense. Friends desire to help each other succeed. If your musicians truly like each other the competitiveness can largely be overcome.

I have seen this principle in action for years in my home church, but have had this idea reinforced as I travel and minister in churches nationwide. I regularly hear stories of musicians' competitive attitudes that have been overcome by those involved becoming friends.

Practically speaking, simply spending time together in non-ministry scenarios can cause this to become reality. An informal dinner together can give people a chance to just talk and become acquainted with one another. A trip to a ball game. A night at the symphony. A worship ministry retreat. All of these can be very helpful in forming stronger relationships and thereby cause them to work together more readily.

Beyond this, cultivating a servant attitude among those involved in the worship ministry will also help musicians on different talent levels to work together. True servanthood is almost an anomaly in our society. Unfortunately, my experience has been that it is even more rare among musicians. However, when musicians begin to see their role as one of serving — serving the pastor, the congregation, even one another — their entire attitude changes. Music ministry becomes a place to demonstrate servanthood instead of being a venue for displaying their talents.

These are just a couple of practical suggestions for getting musicians of varied skill levels to work together. Instilling these ideas into your music ministry can go a long way toward making this concept reality.

Appendix

A Praise and Worship Survey
For the Congregational Members

Part A is designed as a personal analysis of the Sunday morning worship time. It should be understood that there are no right or wrong answers. Your answers, although they may be strongly held opinions, are only opinions.

Part A

1. Do you think we:
   a. do too many slow songs.
   b. do too many fast songs.
   c. have an acceptable balance of slow and fast songs.

2. Do you think we:
   a. learn too many new songs.
   b. do not learn enough new songs.
   c. learn just enough new songs.

3. Do you think the music of the songs we use is overall:
   a. too simple to be challenging.
   b. too difficult to sing.
   c. not too difficult but not too easy.

4. Do you think the lyrics of the songs we use are overall:
   a. too simple to be challenging.
   b. too difficult to sing.
   c. not too difficult but not too easy.

5. Do you think the style of music being used is:
    a. too contemporary.
    b. too traditional.
    c. about right.

6. How do feel about the amount of time spent in worship on Sunday morning?
    a. too long
    b. too short
    c. about right

7. How do you feel about the overall Sunday morning worship experience?
    a. boring
    b. satisfying
    c. _____

Part B is designed to add insights to the answers given in Part A. These questions, although they may be uncomfortable, should be answered as candidly as possible. (Please note that answers to Part A will not be tabulated if Part B is not completed).

Part B

1. When you arrive on Sunday morning are you fully prepared to worship the Lord:
    a. all of the time.
    b. some of the time.
    c. very seldom.

2. Do you:
>   a. enter into worship freely.
>   b. prefer to sit and watch others worship.
>   c. ignore worship and think about other matters.

3. Do you:
>   a. freely express your worship to the Lord.
>   b. need to be coaxed along in worship.
>   c. wait to be compelled to worship God.

4. Do you worship the Lord on your own during the week?
>   a. often.
>   b. occasionally.
>   c. seldom.

5. Do you harbor negative attitudes toward your brothers and sisters in the Lord in the service?
>   a. often
>   b. occasionally
>   c. seldom

6. Do you feel that you could do a better job of leading worship on a consistent basis?
>   Yes/No

Other Books by Tom Kraeuter

Keys to Becoming an Effective Worship Leader

This book has sold over 30,000 copies and continues to be the standard for worship leaders world-wide.

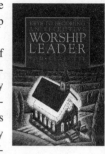

Bill Rayborn of The Church Music Report said this: "In very practical, down-to-earth terms Tom leads you through a journey into the heart of the effective worship leader... a journey needed by us all!"

Developing an Effective Worship Ministry

This is the A - Z book on developing the ministry of praise and worship in the local church. Worship team guidelines, establishing a vision for music ministry, finding the right people, the pastor's role in the worship ministry, etc.

Things They Didn't Teach Me In Worship Leading School

The experiences of 50 prominent worship leaders from around the world packed into one encouraging and insightful book. Includes stories from Graham Kendrick, La-Mar Boschman, Bob Fitts, Steve Fry, and many more.

Worship Is... What?!

Rethinking Our Ideas About Worship

In his usual story-filled way, Tom makes the Scriptures come alive for today. If you want to understand what worship is all about — or if you think you already do — you should read this book.

If Standing Together Is So Great, Why Do We Keep Falling Apart?

The Church in America is missing much of the power of God because of a lack of unity. You'll learn why unity is so vital as well as specific steps of how to make it reality.

ORDER FORM

	QTY	EACH	TOTAL
Worship Is...What?!		$ 8.00	
If Standing Together Is So Great, Why Do We Keep Falling Apart?		$ 8.00	
Things They Didn't Teach Me In Worship Leading School		$10.00	
Keys to Becoming an Effective Worship Leader		$ 8.00	
Developing an Effective Worship Ministry		$ 8.00	
The Worship Leader's Handbook		$ 9.00	
		Subtotal	
Postage/Packaging — 10% of subtotal for U.S. & Canada, minimum $1.50; 40% for overseas			
		TOTAL	

☐ Enclosed is my check for $_____
   made payable to EMERALD BOOKS

PAYMENT OPTIONS

☐ Credit Card — Please bill my:

☐ MC ☐ Visa Credit Card Exp._____

Card#_____

Signature_____

Name_____

_____

Address_____

City_____ ST_____ ZIP_____

Phone_____ E-mail_____

Mail to: Emerald Books • P.O. Box 635 • Lynnwood, WA 98046
Telephone orders (charge cards only) call: (800) 922-2143
Monday through Friday, 8:30 - 4:30 PST